I'LL MAKE YOU AN OFFER YOU CAN'T REFUSE

I'LL MAKE YOU AN OFFER YOU CAN'T REFUSE

Insider Business Tips from a Former Mob Boss

MICHAEL FRANZESE

NELSON BOOKS

An Imprint of Thomas Nelson

Published in Nashville, Tennessee, by Nelson Books, an imprint of Thomas Nelson. Nelson Books and Thomas Nelson are registered trademarks of HarperCollins Christian Publishing, Inc.

Thomas Nelson titles may be purchased in bulk for educational, business, fund-raising, or sales promotional use. For information, please e-mail SpecialMarkets@ ThomasNelson.com.

Scripture quotations, except those on pages 56, 96, 123, 141, and 145, are taken from HOLY BIBLE: NEW INTERNATIONAL VERSION®. © 1973, 1978, 1984 by International Bible Society. Used by permission of Zondervan Publishing House. All rights reserved.

As for the exceptions mentioned above, they are taken from Holman Christian Standard Bible. © 1999, 2000, 2002, 2003 by Broadman and Holman Publishers. All rights reserved.

Niccolò Machiavelli, *The Prince and Other Writings*, trans. Wayne A. Rebhorn (New York: Barnes & Noble Classics, 2003).

Niccolò Machiavelli, *The Prince*, trans. W. K. Marriott, accessed via Project Gutenberg. EText No. 1232 .

Library of Congress Control Number: 2009921620

ISBN 978-1-59555-426-0 (paperback)
ISBN 978-1-59555-163-4 (hardcover)

Printed in the United States of America
HB 08.08.2023

To all of you who have been
blessed with a second opportunity
to succeed in life.
Don't blow it!

CONTENTS

CHAPTER ONE

Mob Up Your Business

Most people don't like reading long quotes. Indulge me:

> CRIME PAYS. Annual gross income from the rackets will
> probably exceed $50 billion this year. That makes the mob's
> business greater than all U.S. iron, steel, copper, and alumi-
> num manufacturing combined, or about 1.1% of GNP.
> These figures, compiled for the President's Commission on
> Organized Crime, include only revenues from traditional
> mob businesses, such as narcotics, loan-sharking, illegal gam-
> bling, and prostitution. They do not include billions more
> brought in from the mob's diversification into such legitimate
> enterprises as entertainment, construction, trucking, and
> food and liquor wholesaling. . . . The organization chart of a
> crime family or syndicate mirrors the management structure
> of a corporation. At the top of the pyramid is a boss, or chief
> executive. Below him are an underboss (chief operating offi-
> cer) and a consigliore (general counsel). Then follow the ranks
> of capos (vice presidents) and soldiers (lower level employees
> who carry out the bosses' orders). Like corporations, crime
> groups often rely on outside consultants. . . . Consultants are

almost as popular with organized crime families as they are with corporations. These special counselors—lawyers, labor experts, and political advisors—shuttle between members of the mob and moviemakers, hotel and casino operators, owners of professional sports franchises, corporate chief executives, and public officeholders. . . ."[1]

Organized crime, a $50 billion annual industry? Revenues greater than U.S. Steel? Consultants, lawyers, and labor experts? A business structure similar to a major corporation?

Tony Soprano, what the heck happened to you?

No doubt about it: The information presented to the President's Commission on Organized Crime paints a far different picture of the mob's business operations than the one portrayed by Tony's sometimes inept crew of not-so-merry "made men."

How do I know? I was a capo in the Colombo crime family when the commission made its report in the 1980s. I can tell you firsthand that Tony and his men may be entertaining, but they miss the mark when it comes to the mob's extensive and complex business dealings. Not to mention that if a real mob boss was caught pouring out his heart to some sexy psychiatrist, you can bet he'd end up in the trunk of a car by the end of the week. At the latest. We didn't reveal our secrets to outsiders, not about business, not about anything. That would be considered a breach of confidence. And breaches of confidence are not tolerated in "the life," more commonly known as La Cosa Nostra, translated from Italian as "this thing of ours."

---

1. Roy Rowan, "The 50 Biggest Mafia Bosses," *Fortune*, 10 November 1986.

Business in "the Life"

Fortune magazine covered the Commission's report. It was 1986, and the editors ranked the fifty biggest mob bosses in terms of wealth and power—like the Fortune 500 for wise-guys. I was one of the mobsters featured in the twelve-page spread. At thirty-five years of age, I held the distinction of being the youngest mobster to make the list. I ranked just five slots below John Gotti. The "Dapper Don" himself was ranked number thirteen, and that was after he allegedly orchestrated the infamous rubout of Gambino family boss "Big Paul" Castellano.

The reporter devoted a full page to summarizing the various operations I controlled and the intricate business scams I was alleged to have masterminded.

I had interests in labor unions, construction, entertainment, and sports. I ran numbers, bookmaking, and loan-sharking operations. I operated auto dealerships and repair shops. I had interests in nightclubs, restaurants, and catering halls. I controlled bankers and accountants. I had vice presidents and CEOs of major corporations on my payroll. I even dabbled in the stock market. And I was the boss of what proved to be *the* most lucrative enterprise the mob had seen since Prohibition, the wholesale gasoline business (more about that later).

My operation was pulling in $6 to $8 million a week, give or take a mil. *Vanity Fair* called me "one of the biggest money earners the mob had seen since Al Capone." Tom Brokaw called me a "prince of the mafia, as rich as royalty." I wonder if Jack Welch would have hired me to run a division of GE, or if I could have gone all the way and survived a season of Trump's

The Apprentice. Oh, well. Life can sometimes be an endless string of blown opportunities.

My dad was happy. Sonny Franzese, my father, was the underboss of the Colombo family. He proposed my membership into the family. At the time, he was serving fifty years in the federal pen for a phony bank-robbery rap. But he was real proud of me as I shot up through the mob ranks, generating money from the streets in the way that Michael Milken was generating money from his junk bonds. Back then, and especially when he was out on parole, we—the mob's elder statesman and its young rising star—were quite the team to be reckoned with.

And there was a reckoning.

Calling It Quits

Former Manhattan U.S. attorney Rudolph Giuliani was the first G-Man to take a shot at me as a made man. He tried pinning a conviction for racketeering on me. Though Giuliani's office was stealing national headlines as the most aggressive gang-busting squad of G-Men since the days of the Southern District's own Thomas Dewey, I managed to beat the case.

Next came Ed McDonald and the Organized Crime Strike Force in Brooklyn. McDonald and his team of FBI special agents had a bull's eye on my back for years. Let me tell you: these guys were relentless. McDonald had managed to make quite a name for himself a few years earlier when he flipped Henry Hill and took down the guys allegedly involved in the infamous Lufthansa robbery at New York's Idlewild Airport (since rechristened JFK International Airport). His accomplishment was so lauded that he was later cast to play himself in the movie *Goodfellas*. McDonald assembled a massive fourteen-agency government team, the "Michael Franzese Task Force." They created a colored chart that outlined my business interests and needed twenty Magic Marker colors to isolate all my streams of income. It took them months to figure out my organization. But they finally linked it all up.

Toward the end of 1985, McDonald hit me and members of my crew with a twenty-eight-count, ninety-eight-page racketeering bombshell. The charges were the garden variety, things like loan sharking, extortion, wire fraud, and labor racketeering. The usual. I had a few additional charges that were unique to my own personal misdeeds, mainly those pertaining to my scheme to defraud Uncle Sam of a few billion dollars in gas-tax money.

It was a complicated scheme that involved a considerable amount of ingenuity to pull off. And it worked like a charm for years. Every gallon sold by the cartel I controlled cost the government thirty-five cents in unpaid taxes. And we sold a lot—a half billion gallons of bootleg gas every month at our peak. We had a near monopoly on independent gas stations in Northeastern and Atlantic seaboard states.

The irony of the scheme was that while the government treasury was being defrauded, the price of gas at the pump went down. With a thirty-five-cent advantage over our major branded competitors, we lowered our prices to the gas stations, which, in turn, lowered their prices to the consumer at the pump. I stole from the rich and passed on the savings to the consumer. A veritable modern-day Robin Hood! Of course, I made sure both myself and the Colombo Family took a healthy cut of the action in the middle.

The Department of Justice didn't consider our beneficia-
ries akin to the poor people of Sherwood Forest. The feds were
onto us. It was only a matter of time before they squeezed
cooperation out of an insider who would eventually bring me
and the enterprise into a federal courtroom to answer charges.
That day came on December 16, 1985, just three days before
the Castellano hit. Having been indicted and tried four times
previously by both state and federal law-enforcement agencies,
and after never being convicted of anything, it appeared I
would be squaring off with the feds for yet a fifth go-round,
this time in a Brooklyn federal courthouse.

"You could beat this rap," I remember my lawyer saying.
"We beat Giuliani; we can beat McDonald too."

But I didn't. I didn't try. I ended it. All of it. I decided to
quit the mob. Easier said than done. How I managed to do that
and live is covered in a previously written book.

Business Is Business

That was then. I did my time and no longer consider myself a
member of organized crime, having renounced the blood oath I
took more than thirty years ago when I was inducted into the
Colombo crime family. I no longer engage in mob-related activities or run multimillion-dollar business operations. That chapter
of my life is closed. *Mostly*.

For the purposes of this book, I want to pull out a few
pages, specifically to share with you what I learned during the
years I managed booming enterprises for the Colombo family.

Some of you might wonder what possible similarities there

are between running a mob enterprise and operating a legitimate business. What can be taken from a mobster's approach to business that can prove beneficial in the straight workplace? After all, mob guys are criminals. They are in the "business" of crime (the operative word being "business").

Organized crime in America has been thriving for almost a century. It has raked in billions of dollars year after year through a plethora of lucrative endeavors—plenty of them clean as a whistle, or pretty close. The mob has extended its influence to almost every industry known throughout the United States, from the stodgy boardrooms of Manhattan, to the spine-tingling sound stages of Hollywood, to the revered halls of our nation's capital. Make no mistake about it. The mob has made its formidable presence known everywhere. Want proof? Just ask the Department of Justice and the various law-enforcement agencies throughout the country that have been trying for decades to strip the mob of its massive web of business interests.

I assure you, none of this has been accomplished by accident. To operate any business successfully, one must possess certain qualities and adhere to a certain philosophy critical to the success of that business. The men who run the business of organized crime are more than qualified to do so. Without ever earning a bachelor's degree, a master's degree, or a PhD, and in many cases without even graduating from high school, mobsters have managed to operate and dominate legitimate businesses having annual revenues in the hundreds of millions of dollars.

Law enforcement will have you believe that this is accomplished through fear and intimidation, by using a gun and a lead pipe instead of PowerPoint and a spreadsheet. In some cases that's true, but in most cases I can tell you it's just not practical to wave a gun in the boardroom. And usually it's not even necessary. Anyone who sells the mob short when it comes to its ingenuity, its ability to connect with people from all walks of life, and its substantial profit margins is simply kidding themselves.

There is no doubt in my mind that many of the mob executives who succeeded in the business of organized crime would have been equally successful in the boardrooms and business offices of corporate America. Mob executives possess unique instincts, a "street sense" that isn't taught in the classrooms at Harvard or the Wharton School of Business. They're acquired through living a lifestyle where almost every day presents a challenge just to survive, where every friend is your potential enemy, where a board meeting just might prove to be your last encounter on earth. Mob executives whose bottom line is penciled in red ink don't get fired. They end up lying in something red. Blood. Their own. Hostile takeovers amount to either racketeering indictments and business seizures from raiders on the outside, or a bloody war waged from traitors within. That's bound to engender a certain knack for survival.

A Caveat

Don't get me wrong. Before we go any further, I want to make it crystal clear that in no way am I suggesting to the readers of this book or to anyone in general that they be involved in any kind of criminal activity, in or out of the workplace. Crime at any level has no place in our society, and I know that better than most. It's destructive, immoral, and harmful to innocent people.

And don't fool yourself: You cannot get away with criminal activity in this country. Not in the long run. For most people not in the short run either. Law enforcement is too sophisticated and has garnered too many technological and legal weapons to fight crime in the streets as well as in the boardrooms. My indictment, conviction, and imprisonment make this point all too well. The federal and state governments have beefed up their arsenals of crime-fighting weapons over the past twenty years, particularly in the area of white-collar crime. White-collar criminals no longer receive a slap on the wrist in a federal courthouse. These days they get hit with a swift, hard kick in the *tuchas*. After all the corporate scandals of the last few years and the financial meltdown of 2008, you can bet that trend will continue.

Often, it's when a corporate executive is least aware that eyes are on him or her. Just ask the boys from Enron and WorldCom who are donning orange cotton instead of Italian suits. Had Dennis Kozlowski been paying a little more attention, he might have figured out that people tend to notice six-thousand-dollar shower curtains. And Martha Stewart might have avoided an extended stay at the fed's country inn had she realized that the diva routine does not bode well with the all-powerful Department of Justice. A little humility on her end when facing the DOJ lawyers might have kept her cooking in the studio kitchen instead of planting seeds in the prison garden.

Finally, in no way is it my intent to glorify organized crime or the mobsters who run it—me included. I'm going to tell you how it is, but I'm also the first guy to tell you the life is bad, and that no one who chooses it should be held in high regard.

No Magic Formula

There is no shortage today of people willing to share their secret formulas for business success. Books on the subject are as plentiful as mob guys at the racetrack. Visit any airport bookstore and you are sure to see the latest offering from the likes of Donald Trump, telling you why he wants you to be rich, how to get rich, and how to find your way to the top. That's right: The Donald will share with you his best-kept secrets.

Well, here's a not-so-well-kept secret about The Donald, one that Trump has in common with a few other famous billionaires, like J. Paul Getty and Howard Hughes Jr. When they were coming up, these guys all inherited huge fortunes from their fathers. The senior Trump amassed a $400 million fortune, which was largely left to his children, forming the bulk of Donald Trump's wealth. Similar story for Getty. "While I did make money—and quite a bit of it—on my own, I doubt if there would be a 'Getty Empire' today if I had not taken over my father's thriving oil business after his death," he wrote in his autobiography. And Hughes? Dad created the fortune that Howard Jr. inherited at the age of eighteen. The company he created, the Hughes Tool Company, when taken public in 1972, earned Howard Hughes Jr. $150 million in one day.

There are exceptions, but a generous number of multi-millionaires, including Bill Gates, got a head start from parents or grandparents. I am not taking anything away from their accomplishments. By all accounts, they were or are very intelligent entrepreneurs who worked hard and made the most of what advantages they were given. But let's be honest: it's hard to take a guy's word on success when his pop bankrolls him to the tune of a few hundred million. Besides, if a guy like Trump really had the secret, would he tell? Not even Tony, on his couch, would spill those beans.

So how do you make it? Trump says, "Everything in life is luck." Getty's closer: "Rise early, work hard, strike oil." Hard work and an early start to the day are helpful for success. I'll talk more about that later. Inheriting the substantial bankroll needed to dig for oil doesn't hurt either. And the success of any business is helped by a stroke of good luck, along with a few hundred million in inheritance. Hardworking, wealthy businesspeople seem to have all the luck.

Best advice? Give up any thought of a magic formula that will guarantee your success. All the infomercials that promise to give you the ten secret steps to wealth beyond your wildest dreams are false advertising. Get real. There are far too many variables in life for any of these schemes to amount to much beyond fat wallets for the infomercial pitchmen and royalty checks for the business book authors. Nothing wrong with that, but don't be a sucker.

There are no shortcuts to success that I am aware of, not even in the world of organized crime. I got something better. In the mob we were always giving one another "tips," like a tip on a certain horse in a certain race at Belmont, a certain basketball player who might have been induced to shave some points in a game, or a load of designer suits that would be falling out of the back of a truck. Quite often, these tips proved to be of real value. So that's what I'm doing here, giving you a few tips, such as:

- the importance of cutting to the chase
- the value of having a good crew and a solid *consigliere*
- what you can learn from reading wiseguys like Machiavelli and Solomon
- why loose lips sink ships (and threaten businesses)
- how to handle yourself in a "sit-down"
- how gambling can trip your business (and your employees, if you've got them)
- what to learn from your failures
- the danger to yourself and your business of bending the rules
- how to think about real success

Whether you're a corporate executive, a small-business owner, or even a college student contemplating business school, these and the other tips I share are going to pay off for years to come.

Of course, a measure of caution is always advisable when acting on a tip, either from a mobster or from a trusted friend or associate. All those who relied on investment tips from Bernie Madoff can attest to that. I can recall a time when I took a greedy corporate executive to "school" after I discovered he was secretly lining his pockets with cash that was supposed to be shared between us. I gave him a tip on a long shot horse that was sure to win in the third race at Roosevelt Raceway on Long Island. (The track has since been demolished.) The horse was a 30–1 long shot. It was one race away from the glue factory, but I told him to bet the house on the nag, and he did. The horse came in dead last. He got the message, and from that point on, I got my money.

But, I can assure you, these tips are legit, and they're sure to pay off.

GET THE MESSAGE

1. There is no magic formula that will guarantee your success.

2. Don't get "schooled." A measure of caution is always advisable when acting on a tip, either from a former mobster or from a trusted friend or associate.

CHAPTER TWO

First, Nail Down the Basics

Ask a mobster to describe the operating plan for his business. He'll probably give you a smirk and reply, "To make money. Whaddaya think?" Take it a step further. Ask him how he intends to do it. He'll probably sigh as though he's got no patience for your question; then he'll pop out his chin and say, "By taking your money." That's supposed to scare you. Stick it out. There's a lot to learn.

Mob guys have the philosophy that all the money in another person's pocket really belongs to them. Their business plan is simple: figure out how to take it from the sucker's pocket and get it into their own. (In mob parlance a *sucker* is anyone not in the life.) This probably won't secure them financing at their local bank, but at least it's a plan. You'd be surprised how many businesspeople I speak to who don't have this figured out yet. First tip of the day: don't field the ball till you've covered your bases.

Get Your Plan

Unless you're the U.S. Mint or a counterfeiter, you are not in business to "make" money. You are in business to "take" it—from anyone willing to buy the product or service that your business is selling. Like the mob guy's, the bottom line to your business plan is to take as much money as you can from your clients' and customers' pockets and get it into yours. And you thought you had nothing in common with the mob. Same end game, different game plan.

Having a clear, focused, written plan for your business is crucial—one based on a simple organizing principle and purpose. It's critical whether you are a long-surviving firm or a fresh-faced startup, whether you manage a business unit in a larger company, or the last-passed buck finally rests on your desk. It helps keep you on track as far as the direction you want your business to take, what your bottom line is, and how you plan to get there. If you need financing, a written business plan will almost always be required by a bank, equity firm, or private lender. You must define the ultimate goals of your business in advance and refer to them as you progress. You can't hit a target you can't see. (That's why mob guys always set their targets at close range.) Have measurable, specific outcomes, and determine the route you must take to get there. It's like DaVinci supposedly said: "Make your work to be in keeping with your purpose." If you don't, you'll end up in trouble.

Business owners tend to get off track and stray from the original plan when things aren't going well. Hit a rough patch and you doubt the original plan. Deviate to grab a buck here or cash in on an opportunity there. Yes, it's important to be flexible with your business plan at times. That's a given. Market trends and economic conditions might require you to alter or tweak your plan every now and again. Depending on what type of trade you're in, you might want to diversify your business, offer additional services, or implement different strategies to increase your company's productivity and profitability.

> I believe also that he will be successful who directs his actions according to the spirit of the times, and that he whose actions do not accord with the times will not be successful.
>
> MACHIAVELLI

But watch out! Unless your plan was a bad one to begin with, the moves you make should be focused around the context of your plan. Think of it as a lodestone, magnetically gripping all your work so you don't spin off course. If it's a good plan and you stick to it, then you'll ride out the bad times and be in a good place when you emerge on the other side.

Mobsters don't need written business plans. For them, the plan is always the same. Get as much money as you can, as fast as you can. They tend not to deviate from that objective. Furthermore, paper trails for mobsters usually end up as evidence in a courtroom. So if you happen to be in the mob, scratch the business plan. For everyone else, start writing.

I don't count on this being obvious anymore, so I'll say it: Make sure it's a good one. When you're known as a money guy on the street, people come to you all the time for some cash, a little backing, a little seed money. I was propositioned every day by people wanting to start a business—everything from restaurants to an insurance company. I always asked wannabe entrepreneurs what the plan was for their business venture. Quite often, I got the "to make money" response. When I asked them to provide a specific blueprint for how their business was actually going to make money, they generally responded with something like, "The same way everyone else in that business is doing it." For the record, that's not a good plan. Nobody with his head up in a cloud gets financing.

Bad business plans are usually the result of bad ideas, and will probably end up as a failed business. That's another reason to put your business plan on paper. It requires you to look at your own plan. Read it over a couple of times. Really think about it. Does it make logistical sense? Is it doable? You should be your own plan's toughest critic and its best defender. Work through the angles, the ins and outs, the contingencies, the what-ifs, anything that's relevant. If it doesn't make sense in theory, it probably will not make sense in practice. Kill it and move on. As a made guy in the Colombo family, I learned it was better to have no business plan than a bad business plan. Bad business plans tend to shorten a mobster's life.

Don't Get Killed in Your Pajamas

Once you've got your plan, you have to work it. And work it hard.

Shortly after being inducted into the family, I was at the Colombo headquarters on Carroll Street in Brooklyn, where I was required to be almost every day during my first year of mob membership. I was sitting with the boss and my caporegime, sipping black coffee and listening intently as they talked about a soldier from another family who had met with his demise the previous morning. Apparently the unsuspecting mobster had been shot and killed by two gunmen as he walked outside his home to retrieve something from his car. It was reported somewhere that he was wearing pajamas. I remember my boss's comment to this day. "What the hell was he doing in his pajamas? He got whacked at eleven o'clock in the morning!" I never forgot that, and I've never owned a pair of pajamas since.

I never met a successful mobster who didn't start his day at the crack of dawn. Of course, that eliminated most of them who didn't normally arrive home until the crack of dawn. Mob guys love the night life. When I was in the life, I spent most weeknights out on the town, often combining business and pleasure at nightclubs and after-hour joints all over Manhattan and Long Island. Managing my extensive business affairs along with dealing with the mob business of my crew was more than a full-time job. But regardless of what time I hit the sack, I was up when the rooster crowed and ready to work. Fifteen- and eighteen-hour workdays were my routine. For those of you who think you can achieve success in business without putting in the time, you better get yourself a drawer full of silk pajamas. That's about the closest to feeling wealthy you're going to get.

There are no magic formulas in business, because real life has too many variables. But from where I'm sitting and from what I've seen, there is at least one common denominator among people who have achieved great success in their business endeavors—hard work. No substitute for it. People who succeed in business do not plan their day around what's easy and convenient. They take what's hard. I am not saying that hard work alone will guarantee success. Remember, as far as I am concerned, there are no guarantees. Hard work is only one ingredient, but it is a primary ingredient. On one hand, I know lots of men and women who work very hard, yet don't achieve any meaningful success. On the other hand, I don't know of anyone who has experienced success without working hard to achieve it. And I'm not talking about people who win the lottery or who have inherited money. Silver spoons don't count.

I have met many people, mobsters included, who want to be in business because they believe being the boss means more money and less work. No way that's true (unless, of course, they have a no-show union job—I know about those guys). My father once told me, "Mike, when you're in business, ya gotta watch everything that's going on. Ya gotta have eyes in the back of your head." (Of course mob guys need eyes in the backs of their heads, just in case there's a guy back there with a .38 revolver. So that came natural to us.) Bottom line: The boss has to have his eyes focused on more than anyone else. If he starts slacking, someone's going to yank the slack out of his rope, let me tell you.

The late Green Bay Packer coach Vince Lombardi knew a thing or two about this: "The harder you work," he said, "the harder it is to surrender." He knew the harder his team worked on the practice field, the more likely they were to give everything they had on the field on game day. There would be no surrender. Victory would have to be taken from them. They would prevail, no matter what the challenge. Business owners, like football players, are faced with challenges all the time. Financial pressures can beat you down and choke you up. Those pressures can get so bad you want to close up shop. But the harder you work to build your business, the less likely you are to give in to the pressure. Dig in. Hard work builds character, and strong character makes strong leaders and businesspeople.

Hard work is also important for another, related reason: it's a proxy for how seriously you take what you do. If you poke around the edges of your business or dabble in this or that, I'll give your eventual failure almost any odds you want. The conscientious usually beat the dabblers. Show me someone with a simple plan, who works it hard, and I'll show you someone focused on making his business succeed.

But don't be stupid about it. One of your top goals in working hard to achieve success should be to provide for your quality of life. Being in business is about having the freedom to enjoy your life. Becoming a slave to your work is defeating one of the ultimate purposes you are working to fulfill. Be smart in your approach to climbing the ladder. I'll say more about this in the final chapter, but for now, make sure you leave time for other areas of your life that are important—like family, friends, and faith.

And remember, if you pull a Tony Soprano and walk outside for the morning paper, don't do it in your pajamas.

Cut to the Chase

So you've got your plan, and you're working it hard. Make sure you also work it well. We all know the picture: disorganized, harried businessperson running around like a chicken with his head cut off. I have never seen or heard of a made man doing that. (I know of a former mobster whose nickname was "Chicken Head," but that was because of his penchant for shooting off the heads of birds to improve his marksmanship.) Mobsters like to keep business matters simple. Their motto is "Cut to the chase." They believe in eliminating the clutter. They want a clear and easy path to the cash.

Mobsters were using the "show me the money" line long before it was made famous in *Jerry Maguire*. But a mobster's eagerness to cut to the chase and see the money is *not* always in the best interests of a business. As most mob guys are not interested in the long-term growth of a business, they usually want to see all the money, and leave very little for the business to operate. This is not advisable for the legitimate business-person. But once again, mobsters get it half right, and it usually works for them.

If your business plan lays out your goals, then you'll want to get to them with as little friction as possible. Following every rabbit, answering every call, putting off for tomorrow what can be done right this minute—this is a recipe for disaster. All that is clutter. Head clutter. Life clutter. It's going to block you from reaching your goals. Cut it out. You got to cut to the chase.

Let me tell you about a famous businessman who cuts to the chase. Keeps his routine simple. He's been doing it this way for more than forty years and happens to be the second wealthiest person in the country, with a net worth of several billion dollars. He most certainly has been shown the money. He is none other than the Oracle of Omaha himself, Warren Buffett. Talk about keeping it simple. Consider this: The genius stock investor arrives at his Berkshire Hathaway offices at 8:30 a.m. He rarely attends meetings, doesn't check e-mails (there's no computer on his desk), and he doesn't talk on the phone much. Before making a stock purchase, Buffett might consult with his longtime confidant and Berkshire vice chairman, Charles Munger.

The company he has run for more than four decades is huge, yet his personal system of operation is pretty barebones.

Buffett keeps things simple and does what he does best—buy and sell stock. He doesn't get sidetracked. He stays within his circle of competence. He doesn't run around his offices like a chicken without a head, worrying about matters he has hired others to manage. He has created a structure within his company that allows him to maintain control of his business without having to be in a manic state.

It would be wise for you, the businessperson, to cut to the chase Buffett-style. Getting worked up, trying to micromanage every little detail of your business, and being in a perpetual state of frenzy will often prevent you from achieving the very success you are trying to obtain. Slow down. Take a breath. Eliminate the clutter on your desk and in your head. Stick to the original plan and don't operate your business in a panic. Create a structure in your business that allows you to *eat* your chicken—cacciatore-style—and not *act* like one.

That said, there will be times when conditions arising in your business will require quick action. A marketing program that is not working, an employee not fulfilling his responsibilities, the discovery that you are carrying an inferior product, improper pricing, inefficient accounting procedures, or even an unclean workplace—all examples of conditions that can hurt your business. Timidity repays trouble with interest. Business owners must act before one problem leads to others—especially when conditions don't correct themselves. Action must be taken to prevent further damage. But again, if you have *kept things simple* all along, making a regular habit of cutting to the chase, then when a problem does arise, you will be able to quickly and efficiently put out that fire—*before* it becomes the "Towering Inferno."

Ya Gotta Have a Crew

Here's an old adage: "You're only as good as the people you have around you." Here's another one: "Lie down with dogs and you're gonna get fleas." To achieve success in business, it is imperative that you assemble the right crew to support your efforts. Buffett can't do what he does without his crew. Neither can you. No way around it.

> Two are better than one, because they have a good return for their work.
>
> SOLOMON

> [T]he first opinion which one forms of a prince, and of his understanding, is by observing the men he has around him; and when they are capable and faithful he may always be considered wise, because he has known how to recognize the capable and to keep them faithful. But when they are other-wise one cannot form a good opinion of him, for the prime error which he made was in choosing them.
>
> MACHIAVELLI

A leader's staff can make him or her appear much more intelligent than he or she really is—or they can make the leader appear thoroughly incompetent. And forget mere appearances. A good crew is the best evidence that you *are* intelligent and competent and gives you a fighting chance in executing your plan. Got a bad crew? Fuggedaboutit.

A few things to keep in mind. You've got to have guys who are capable, reliable, and most important, honest.

Honesty. I was introduced to the wholesale gasoline business by a man named Lawrence Iorizzo. Larry was a whale of a man, standing six foot four and weighing a whopping 450 pounds. As an integral member of my operation, the big man easily met the first two criteria. He was extremely capable and very reliable. We went on to make millions of dollars together selling bootleg gasoline. But honest? I found out years later that Larry kept a file of all the illegal activity he believed I had engaged in over the eight years we worked together. Knowing I was a prize catch for the feds, I would be his "Get Out of Jail Free card" were he ever to run afoul of the law. And years later he used that file for just that purpose. Although I was acquitted in the only case in which he testified, he still managed to cut a sweetheart deal for himself with the feds. Of course had I been operating my business legally, the file would have been of little value to the feds. It would have been empty. Is anyone keeping a mental file on your business activities?

Honesty does matter in business, even among thieves.

Capability. In the early '70s I purchased a Mazda dealership in Hempstead, Long Island. For years I worked hard turning around a franchise that had been left for dead in the wake of its trademark Wankel engine vehicles. But my blood oath to La Cosa Nostra brought with it much added responsibility, and in time I could no longer effectively handle the day-to-day responsibilities of managing the dealership. In the mob, when your boss summons you, you drop whatever you are doing and go. Customers, suppliers, and employees run a distant second to a mob boss with a bad attitude. Since I could not replace myself in the ranks of the Colombo family, I needed to find a suitable replacement to run the dealership. In steps David Edreich, general manager extraordinaire, to run the dealership in my place. Although he consulted with me on major decisions, I gave him full control over the operation. Not only did he expand the business with innovative sales ideas, but he also won me a ten-day trip to the Orient for placing first in our district in a Mazda Motors–sponsored sales contest. Surrounding yourself with capable people makes you money; it also makes you look smart. Do what you do best, and delegate the rest.

Reliability. Let me tell you about reliability. Back in the day, "Frankie Gangster" was a member of my crew. He was so named because of his outright love of being a gangster. (Mobsters aren't very creative when it comes to picking nicknames. For example, Thomas "Tommy Sneakers" Cacciopoli liked sneakers. John "Jackie Nose" Damico had his big nose fixed. Robert "Bobby the Jew" Epifania looked Jewish. Vincent "Vinny Hot" Decongilio inherited his name from his father, "Freddy Hot." Mob guys like to keep things simple.) When Giuliani indicted me and a number of my crew for racketeering in 1984, Frankie Gangster was *not* listed. The day after I bailed out of the federal lockup, he showed up at my home in Long Island and was very disturbed. "Hey chief," I remember him saying, "why wasn't I arrested with the rest of the crew?" Frankie was actually upset that he was not indicted. He felt left out. Now, that's deep! I can't name another mob guy who was ever upset for being *left out* of an indictment, especially a federal racketeering one.

Although Frankie was a bit off in his thinking, he was a reliable gangster, and I could depend on him to take care of much of the day-to-day administrative work that went along with my being a caporegime in the family. I let him do whatever I thought he did best. Reliability is a key factor to any effective crew member. I relied on Frankie to take care of much of the everyday minutiae that comes with running a mob crew. You know, like collecting the "vig" (interest) from a deadbeat shylock customer or from a gambler who didn't pay up after the big game. I even trusted him to find me a house in Florida, and he found me a gem, on the water in Delray Beach. I liked the house so much I instructed Frankie to make the sellers an offer they couldn't refuse. I wanted the house and everything in it, including the toaster. The sellers initially balked at my request, but cash talks, and two days later they were on a boat to the Bahamas, where they used their newfound fortune to open a restaurant. Frankie G was one reliable gangster.

Enlist a Consigliere

It's not enough to have a crew. You need a *consigliere*. That's the Italian word for an adviser or counselor. The term was made famous in the outside world by *The Godfather*. Robert Duvall played the role of Tom Hagen, the dutiful consigliere to the powerful family don, Vito Corleone. But long before Tom Hagen was dispatched to Los Angeles to make movie producer Jack Woltz an offer he couldn't refuse, Mafia bosses since the days of Lucky Luciano were consulting their consiglieres on matters concerning the family business. A consigliere is an official position of La Cosa Nostra, and the appointee is usually the boss's handpicked, trusted advisor and wields significant power within the family. A heck of a lot more than did Tom

Hagen, who, by the way, was not of Italian descent and therefore could not have held that position in the real mob world.
(Gotta be a *paisan* to earn that button.)

> Make plans by seeking advice; if you wage war, obtain
> guidance.
>
> SOLOMON

Mob bosses understand the importance of seeking wise
counsel from someone they trust in managing the business of
the mob. Government leaders almost always have a consigliere. Jim Baker was a consigliere to both the Bush presidents. Prominent entertainers often use the services of a
consigliere to help them make important business decisions—
which scripts to take, gigs to play, shows to avoid, etc. Agents
and directors may have their own agendas, so it is not unusual
for in-demand entertainers to seek the opinions of a trusted
consigliere before signing any commitments or contracts.

My father served as my advisor on mob business. I found it
very helpful to have a second, more objective opinion before I
acted on certain matters, particularly those of great importance.
I didn't always listen to him. My dad and I weren't always on the
same page when it came to business matters. But even when we
disagreed, I found it valuable to consider my father's well-
informed advice and counsel before I made an executive
decision.

A few things to keep in mind about choosing a consigliere:
A mob consigliere is supposed to be devoid of ambition. This
makes him more likely to render advice based on what is in
the best interest of the business—not anyone else's, including

the boss's. Likewise, your consigliere shoud be a fair and impartial advisor and can be your best friend, a relative, your spouse, a trusted employee, or a hired gun. When you choose your consigliere, make sure he or she

- knows enough of the ins and outs of your business to render a relevant opinion
- can be trusted to give advice in the best interests of your business
- will never flatter you
- will stand up to you when he or she feels you are not acting in the best interest of the business

A consigliere is a safeguard to your own shortsightedness, lack of information or perspective, even your own bad judgment. Get one and use him or her to the maximum.

In the mob we were always cooking up new schemes to take money. But you can only work the more elaborate deals and scams if you're covering the basics: protection, extortion, gambling. Covering the basics means you're standing on firm ground from which to operate—same in mob life as legit life. Get a plan, work it hard, work it efficiently, and get people around you who can help you implement it. Do that and you'll be ready to deliver an offer the recipient can't refuse.

GET THE MESSAGE

1. Have a clear, focused, written plan for your business with measurable, specific outcomes and the route you will take to get there.

2. If you think you can achieve success in business without putting in the time, you better get yourself a drawer full of silk pajamas. That's about the closest to feeling wealthy that you're going to get. People who have achieved great success in their business endeavors take what they do seriously and work hard to make it happen.

3. Get to your business goals with as little friction as possible. Don't let the head clutter block you from reaching your goals. Putting off for tomorrow what can be done right now is a recipe for disaster. Cut it out. You got to cut to the chase.

4. Assemble the right crew to support your efforts—capable, reliable, and most important, honest people.

5. Get a consiglier who can be fair and impartial, but who won't flatter you just to get ahead. You need someone who knows how to stand up to you when he or she feels that you are not acting in the best interest of the business. This can be your best friend, a relative, your spouse, a trusted employee, or a hired gun.

CHAPTER THREE

Next, Beware Machiavelli's Trap

n the last chapter I quoted from two famous business phi-
losophers—Machiavelli and Solomon. This chapter and the
next one are about why.

The Mob's Champion

During my tenure as a soldier and capo in the Colombo crime
family, when a made man went to prison, he was given a reading
assignment: the works of sixteenth-century Italian philosopher
and diplomat Niccolò di Bernardo dei Machiavelli.

Why Machiavelli? For starters, he was Italian, and most wise-
guys believe that Italians are the best at everything in life. There
were no greater ballplayers than Joe DiMaggio, Tony Lazzeri, and
Yogi Berra. The greatest chefs are Italian. You going to tell me
Mario Batali doesn't have a few things figured out? Nothing
compares to Italian opera. Michelangelo was the greatest artist,
sculptor, and poet of all time. DaVinci was the most diversely
talented person who ever lived. Frank Sinatra was the greatest

crooner in all of popular music. If that wasn't enough, the Genoese, Venetians, and the Florentines were the original capitalists—and the best businessmen of their day. Get my drift?

Machiavelli's pedigree made him immediately acceptable to the mob, but it was his philosophy that made him its champion. He is a figure of the Italian Renaissance, widely known for his political treatise *The Prince*, in which he described how a ruler can maintain control of his kingdom. He also explained which princes are the most successful in obtaining and maintaining power. The Machiavellian philosophy is the cornerstone on which La Cosa Nostra, as I knew and lived it, was built. *The Prince* is to the mob as the Bible is to Christians.

Thumb through *The Prince*. You can see that Machiavelli's philosophy for obtaining and maintaining power boils down to "the ends justify the means."

[I]n the actions of all men . . . one judges by the result.

MACHIAVELLI

Any evil action can be justified if it is done for a good purpose. The result, the end, is all that ultimately matters. Although Machiavelli placed restrictions on evil actions, he most certainly did advocate them. He went on to justify those actions in such a way as to make them morally acceptable and not appear to be totally evil in nature. For example, Machiavelli's criterion for engaging in cruel and severe actions was that they be inflicted "at one stroke so as not to have to repeat them daily." The mob might have strayed a bit from that criterion at times, but you get the point.

I first read *The Prince* in 1987 while serving time in the

federal prison at Terminal Island, California. I recognized everything. It was like reading La Cosa Nostra's playbook. It brought
to mind so many of the principles I learned from the mob's
elder statesman. Principles that all members had to live by and
oftentimes die by, such as:

- "[M]en ought either to be well treated or crushed,
  because they can avenge themselves of lighter injuries,
  of more serious ones they cannot; therefore the injury
  that is to be done to a man ought to be of such a kind
  that one does not stand in fear of revenge."
- "[I]njuries ought to be done all at one time, so that,
  being tasted less, they offend less; benefits ought to be
  given little by little, so that the flavour of them may last
  longer."
- "It . . . is much safer to be feared than loved."

Is it any wonder psychologists use the term *Machiavellianism*
to describe a person's desire to deceive and manipulate others
for personal gain?

Machiavelli's ways were my ways. An example: As I mentioned earlier, I controlled a multimillion-dollar gasoline cartel
whose various companies were licensed to sell gasoline wholesale to distributors and retailers up and down the Atlantic seaboard. Competition was fierce. My primary competitors were
major oil companies. The cartel's profits were tied directly to
the volume of gasoline sold. The more gas that flowed out of
the company's pumps, the bigger the profit. The game plan
was to absorb as many competing companies into my operation as possible. Obviously, we weren't going to swallow up

the multibillion-dollar oil conglomerates. Companies such as Mobil, Shell, Exxon, and British Petroleum were well out of reach. But every other competing company was fair game. I'll amplify Machiavelli's quote so you can see my thinking more clearly:

> If he acquires a state [sells a product] he should absorb the surrounding states [companies marketing the same product] and identify his enemies.
>
> MACHIAVELLI

The Machiavellian philosophy provided for a "defeat my enemies at all costs" approach to succeeding. The chief enemy of the mob was the United States Department of Justice. The primary enemies and chief competitors of my business were the major oil companies. In devising an intricate scheme to defraud the government its tax revenue, my associates and I managed to inflict damage on both of my enemies while simultaneously and dramatically increasing the cartel's volume of sales.

> A prince should have no objective but war [to beat the competition].
>
> MACHIAVELLI

The tax money my company stole from the government, as much as forty cents a gallon, provided me with a significant advantage over my competitors. I was able to sell gasoline to station owners, distributors, and other wholesalers at a price even the major oil companies couldn't compete with. The height of my operation saw gasoline spilling out of the company tankers at the rate of half a billion gallons per month. At a minimum of five cents per gallon that was diverted from Uncle Sam's pockets to the company's coffers, the profit was substantial. Do the math!

Double-Edged Sword

But you've got to do more than the math. Do the morals. In the last chapter we talked about having a plan. Now we're talking about how you put it into action. In our current business climate, this discussion is more important than ever. And if we'd had it before the storms hit, the winds might have blown a different direction.

The philosophy a person lives by will probably be the same with which he conducts his business. A person doesn't live his or her life one way, then conduct a business in another. You may try to separate your business from your personal life, but we are still the same person conducting both. That was certainly true in my case. You are who you are at work or at play.

That's why you have to watch out for Machiavelli's trap. People operate with Machiavelli's philosophy because it works. Simple. One scholar introduced *The Prince* by commenting, "Machiavelli was undoubtedly a man of great observation, acuteness, and industry. . . . *The Prince* is bestrewn with truths that can be proved at every turn." But there's also an internal dynamic in the philosophy that will chew you up. I'll explore that as we go on.

Here's an example: Machiavelli's philosophy, as applied in the mob, almost guarantees that a made man's success in business will result in his downfall. I can tell you from experience that success in the world of organized crime is a double-edged sword. Here's how it works. The structure of the mob provides for a member or associate's business to be taken over by the family should he be booted off to prison, commit a grave offense against the family or one of its members, or meet with his demise, timely or otherwise. Surround yourself with men who live by the philosophy that "the end justifies the means" and who share an inherent desire to deceive and manipulate others for personal gain, and you'll find yourself swimming in a pool of bloodthirsty sharks. The philosophy isn't meant to be used on members. But mob guys can be very cunning in concealing their true intent. These are professional criminals we are talking about. When money and power are at stake, honor among thieves is grossly exaggerated. I learned that firsthand.

During my time in the life I had legitimate business interests, including automobile dealerships, leasing companies, auto body repair shops, restaurants, nightclubs, movie production and distribution companies, a general contracting company, a travel agency, and a video store. I also had illegal and silent interests in businesses that included loan-shark operations, labor-union affiliations, gambling, a talent agency, a sports agency, and the aforementioned interest in a wholesale gasoline conglomerate comprised of eighteen different companies. I was aggressive and knew how to use the life to benefit my business pursuits.

When a made man acquires an interest in a business, whether legitimate or illegitimate, he is required to put that interest "on record" with his caporegime if he is a soldier, or with the boss if he is a caporegime. This guarantees that no other made man from within his own family or a rival family can ever lay claim to that business interest. Putting it on record protected his interest from a potential marauding mobster. If a made guy made a claim on an interest that belonged to another and it wasn't on record, the penalty for such an omission could be severe; the mobster holding title to the business might very well lose his interest to the marauding mobster for his infraction. Would have made Machiavelli proud.

But there was another reason for requiring a mobster's business to be on record. The reporting requirement assured the family boss of receiving his end of all the cash flowing into his subordinate's coffers. (Multilevel marketing!) Should that mobster happen to violate the rules or be sent to prison, either kick or have his bucket kicked, the family could easily identify and assume that mobster's business interests, lock, stock, and barrel. Think of it as the mob's version of a will or a life insurance policy with the family boss as the beneficiary. And you thought the mob didn't take care of its own.

> Politics have [business has] no relation to morals.
>
> MACHIAVELLI

The more my business empire grew, the more respect and courtesy I was given as an "earner" for the family. I also had to be more careful not to slip up and have it all taken away. Envy and treachery are as much a part of La Cosa Nostra as is a bowl of linguini with clams. The Machiavellian philosophy for success in both the mob life and in its business demanded that one's instincts remain sharp at all times. I learned that early on. In the mob life, you survive by never taking anyone or anything for granted.

Flawed Philosophy

Certain strategies of Machiavelli, although questionable in intent and morality, can be applicable to the world of legitimate business. In fact, they have enabled some folks to enjoy substantial success in their ventures. Notable examples of strategy from *The Prince* that can be of value to an executive or business owner are:

> [I]njuries [raising prices, cutbacks] ought to be done all at one time, so that, being tasted less, they offend less; benefits [grants, charitable works, raises, bonuses, perks] ought to be given little by little, so that the flavour of them may last longer.

> Whoever desires to found a state [company, business] and gives its laws must start with assuming that all men [other executives, competitors, shareholders] are bad and ever ready to display their vicious nature whenever they may find occasion for it.

> A prince [executive, shop owner] who is not wise himself cannot take wise advice.

There is no doubt that some of Machiavelli's teachings can help one be successful in the very challenging world of business. Henry Ford was thought to have followed the Machiavellian strategy when developing his company into one of America's corporate giants. Other Goliaths of industry have (knowingly or unknowingly) also succeeded under his methodology as well.

La Cosa Nostra has survived and prospered in America for nearly a century adhering largely to the Machiavellian philosophy of obtaining and maintaining power. Throughout the past century, its presence has been felt in nearly every area of legitimate business. And it has been a leading innovator in creating lucrative illegal schemes and enterprises ever since the days of Prohibition and speakeasies. Although the mob as a whole has survived and prospered as a way of life and as a business enterprise (as defined in a RICO indictment), the individual casualties to its members have been nothing short of shocking and devastating. If a made man dies of old age and in his home rather than in a prison cell, he has really accomplished something.

The Machiavellian philosophy for life is seriously flawed. It has elements that are true and pragmatic. That's the bait in the trap. But it creates an atmosphere of deceit, mistrust, and treachery—a place where fear masquerades as loyalty. Eventually, any group of people that adheres to such a philosophy will destroy itself from within. When their enemies discover that the strength of the organization is based on the fear of its members, all they need to do is become the ones who are more feared. The loyalty will vanish into thin air, and the poison-tipped spike in Machiavelli's trap of power and control will be revealed.

By thinking about business primarily in terms of acquiring more and maintaining it whatever the costs, the Machiavellian philosophy also encourages people to lose sight of what's truly important and what's really in their business's best interest. A current example of this is the financial market's multitrillion-dollar trading of credit derivatives known as *credit default swaps* (CDS). These nifty little instruments were created by a young Cambridge University math student at the behest of the bigwigs at JPMorgan Chase bank in New York. In a nutshell, they are bets between two parties as to whether or not a third party (the company) will default on its debt, which is usually in the form of bonds. The party betting the company will perform on its obligations (the seller) sells "protection" to the company betting against its performance (the buyer). For a hefty monthly premium, the seller guarantees the buyer a substantial payoff if the company defaults on its debt within a specified period of time. So let's say a hedge fund wants to increase its profits. The fund managers could sit back and collect a half million dollars a year in protection money for selling protection on a risky junk bond it funded—kind of like an insurance company, except there is no requirement for any asset to back the seller's guarantee.

A CDS is basically used to speculate on market changes. It's a gamble. In most cases, the seller is selling air, collecting free money—free until the bond actually goes into default. Then the hedge fund could be on the hook for a hundred million in claims. But what if the seller of protection doesn't have the hundred million? You get the picture? Everybody loses. It would be like the mob collecting protection money from a business owner it couldn't protect. Of course, that would never happen, because the mob collects the money to protect the business owner against—you guessed it—the mob. You pay, you get protection; you don't, you get shaken down or firebombed, or you suddenly have a union shop.

Warren Buffett once described CDSs as "financial weapons of mass destruction." He was right. These largely bogus financial instruments were conjured up in an effort to raise the bottom line of corporate balance sheets and line the pockets of greedy executives. (If the mob had created such an instrument, the scheme would have been a RICO indictment waiting to happen.) Today, as more and more junk bonds go into default by major U.S. corporations, the devastating impact of this financial tsunami is measured in the loss of business and personal wealth to the tune of trillions of dollars worldwide. So, as you see, greed is Machiavellian and ultimately results in both personal and corporate destruction.

It's not a new story. I ultimately lost or surrendered every business interest I had by following Machiavelli's philosophy during my years in the life. When I went to prison and eventually defected from the life, losing it all became inevitable. I'll talk more about greed later on.

What Really Matters

The manner in which you live your life—your character and integrity—will ultimately be reflected in the way you run your business, and this might very well matter to your potential consumers or clients. Furthermore, the philosophy you adopt to run your business will have as much an impact on the quality of your life as will your company's level of success or failure. Integrity and ethics matter in life as well as in business. Trust me here. This is coming from a guy who had a very flawed concept of both. I suffered as a result, and so did my family.

You're in business to succeed. For most of you that means the ultimate goal is improving the quality of your life. What that doesn't mean is succeeding at all costs by any means. That path will end up destroying your quality of life. Winning is important. Success is important. They provide you with the means to do the things you could not otherwise do in life. Live in a nice home, drive a nice car, enjoy a vacation now and then. You get the picture. But how you win and how you succeed will determine if you get to enjoy the fruits of both with a clear and healthy conscience.

GET THE MESSAGE

1. If you operate under Machiavelli's philosophy "the end justifies the means," beware the double-edged sword.

2. Creating an atmosphere of deceit, mistrust, and treachery in your business—a place where fear masquerades as loyalty—will eventually destroy it from within. When your enemies discover that the strength of your organization is based upon the fear of its members, all they need to do is become the ones who are more feared.

3. Your character and integrity will ultimately be reflected in the way you run your business—this might matter to your potential consumers or clients.

4. The philosophy you adopt to run your business will have as much an impact on the quality of your life as will your company's level of success or failure.

CHAPTER FOUR

Use Solomon's Solution

When mob guys are in jail, they read Machiavelli. When average joes are in the can, they read the Bible. I got pinched on a questionable parole violation in the early nineties, did a stretch for it, and read—of all things—the book of Proverbs. Don't worry. This isn't about religion. The writer of the Proverbs (most of them have been ascribed to King Solomon of ancient Israel) has a lot to say about business and operating in the current market climate.

Solomon: The Original Wiseguy

If your ultimate goal is to achieve and maintain success in business, pitch an ear in Solomon's direction. His proverbs provide a solid framework of values within which business strategies should be implemented. He starts by providing his own mission statement and purpose in giving us his writings:

... for attaining wisdom and discipline; for understanding words of insight; for acquiring a disciplined and prudent life, doing what is right and just and fair.

SOLOMON

Businesspeople would be smart to pay attention. Managers need to exercise *wisdom* in employing strategies that will affect their company's performance and overall operation. They need to be *disciplined* and not reckless in, among other things, managing company funds. They need to be *insightful* in understanding market trends that could affect the current and future growth of their company.

Contrary to popular belief, a *prudent* business manager does not often "gamble" and hope for a lucky outcome. You take a risk after carefully considering all available and relevant information. It's called a calculated risk for a reason. That way your chances of getting "lucky" are significantly increased. Compare that with the housing speculators and credit default swappers who helped tank the market in 2008 looking for an easy win.

Being *right and just and fair* in dealing with business partners and employees is not only smart: it's crucial to a company's long-term success. Even the mob will agree with that. In fact, section 4.2 of La Cosa Nostra's bylaws clearly states:

Made men will treat one another in a fair and just manner at all times. Violation of this policy by any member will not be tolerated and will result in that member's immediate expulsion from the family or in his being "whacked," whichever is less likely to lead to an indictment. This policy will be strictly enforced.

I'm kidding—at least about the bylaws. Up to you to figure out where the joke ends.

Being *right and just and fair* in dealing with customers and clients is obviously important to the success of any business. As the popular saying goes, "The customer is always right." (Unless, of course, he's a royal pain in the butt. That's when you tell him to get lost!)

Doing what is right and just and fair is totally subjective, depending on who is minding the store. Solomon and Machiavelli would not have formed an ideal partnership in that regard. But the benefit of siding with Solomon is that he'll keep you out of Machiavelli's trap covered in the previous chapter.

King Solomon vs. Machiavelli

Solomon's writings have as strong an impact on me today as did Machiavelli's philosophy when I joined La Cosa Nostra. We do what we do within the framework of our philosophies. When I was in the mob, mine was pure Machiavellian. Win at all costs. The end justifies the means. Men should be either treated generously or destroyed. In his teachings, Solomon offered me an alternative to the take-no-prisoners approach advocated by Machiavelli.

> Dishonest money dwindles away, but he who gathers money
> little by little makes it grow.
>
> SOLOMON

Bankruptcy courts, prisons, and cemeteries are filled with

people who engaged in dishonest and illegal business practices. Dishonest gains come with a price. Normally a lot more than the business or its management can bear.

Solomon's teachings are directly opposed to many of Machiavelli's. In *The Prince*, Machiavelli declared that the man who "abandons what is done for what ought to be done, learns his ruin rather than his preservation." Machiavelli admitted that he was a political realist and found conventional standards of morality useless as practical advice. Since so many people fail to act according to these standards in reality, he argued, continuing to be "good" can only weaken a ruler. Instead, he wrote, "it is necessary for a prince . . . to learn how not to be good" according to the circumstances. In other words, be dishonest when you have to. Lie; steal; cheat; do whatever is necessary to gain an advantage, and justify your actions according to the circumstances you are in. Machiavelli said a prince should always seem to have virtues—even if he actually doesn't have any. Appearing virtuous is better than being virtuous, because the prince picks up the benefit of looking good while not having to actually be good. Unconstrained by virtue, a prince can do what he needs to do in any situation. He has no limits, no bounds, no rules. He must, Machiavelli wrote, have a mind "disposed to turn itself about as the winds," able to do good when he can but also do evil when he must. Still, even though on the inside he is able to scheme, he should "appear to him who sees and hears him altogether merciful, faithful, humane, upright, and religious." For Machiavelli, businesses operate as if anything goes as long as you achieve your goals. For Solomon, honesty, integrity, and hard work were the cornerstones of a successful business model.

Some examples from Solomon's maxims about hard work:

- "Diligent hands will rule, but laziness ends in slave labor."
- "All hard work brings a profit, but mere talk leads only to poverty."
- "Do not love sleep or you will grow poor; stay awake and you will have food to spare."

Bill Gates averages just two vacation days a year. Canadian communications mogul Ted Rogers, now seventy-four years old, is a notorious workaholic. Thomas Edison said genius is 1 percent inspiration and 99 percent perspiration. Henry Ford said nobody can think straight who does not work. Idleness warps the mind. I agree. I didn't generate millions of dollars a week sipping on black coffee in a social club on Carroll Street.

How about bad debts? Ever been burned by guaranteeing a loan for somebody? Ever pledged your assets for a loan you weren't sure you could repay? You might have avoided those problems if you'd run across Solomon a little earlier:

- "He who puts up security for another will surely suffer, but whoever refuses to strike hands in pledge is safe."
- "Do not be a man who strikes hands in pledge or puts up security for debts; if you lack the means to pay, your very bed will be snatched from under you."

Things haven't changed much in the past three thousand years. An untold number of businesses are lost every year by taking on debt they can't pay. The housing crisis was precipitated by this very problem. We have seen both Fannie Mae and Freddie Mac, mired in a pool of massive debt, become the recipients of a multibillion-dollar government bailout. AIG, Lehman Brothers, Countrywide Mortgage, and Washington Mutual Bank, all financial behemoths, have collapsed under the weight of debt-laden cement shoes. And their collapse was only the tip of the debt-frozen iceberg. The CEOs of the Big Three North American automakers flew to Washington on their companies' private jets to petition Congress for a multibillion-dollar bailout, and left with a harsh rebuke from Congress to come back when they had a plan. And while there may be other circumstances that led to the Big Three's current financial quagmire, the bottom line is that these companies have taken on more debt than they can pay.

And by the way, when all the trouble is isolated, it's easy to dismiss Solomon's advice. What's a little default here or there? But as you can see from the plight of the Big Three, the system appears to be cracking at the foundations. Defaults frequently have a snowball effect on a business and, at times, an entire industry. The residential real-estate market is now on life support, home foreclosures are at a twenty-year high, and bankruptcy filings are jamming the court dockets. Credit is harder to obtain than a mobster's parole. Mortgage companies, banks, and investment houses are going down faster than a mob boss in a RICO indictment. We're still reeling from the shock, and it's going to take years to sort itself out.

Mob guys love to loan money to businesspeople in trouble. The loans are always high-interest and secured but rarely documented with Universal Commercial Code filings on the business. Notes and mortgages are not necessary. The understanding between lender and borrower is clear. Default and your bed might be the only thing that is not snatched from under you. And though banks and so-called legitimate lenders employ different techniques than mob guys, they can be pretty cold when it comes to foreclosing on security when a loan is in default.

It's About Having and Using Wisdom, Not a Guarantee

Solomon won't make you rich. There is no one secret that explains the success of a wealthy person's business interests. Each person's blueprint is unique. However, each successful business works within a framework, and Solomon offers a solid structure and some brilliant principles upon which you can work to build your company's success.

> Hold on to instruction, do not let it go; guard it well, for it is your life.
>
> SOLOMON

I travel quite a bit, and I can tell you that how-to books on business jam-pack the shelves of just about every airport bookstore in every major city in the country. I have read more than a handful and leafed through many others. My take? They all say pretty much the same thing, just in different ways. There is a plethora of five or ten or twenty steps in these texts that will guarantee your success in business and help you become a millionaire, own a Mercedes Benz or two, and live in a mansion. They might as well be written by the same author. Up to you to figure out if any of the advice is worth the price tag.

Yet, in spite of all this "advice," even the United States is on the verge of defaulting on its debt. Who the heck is minding the store? Apparently not enough businesspeople are visiting airports and reading books. Either that or the authors' guarantees of success are about as valuable as Bear Stearns stock. The reality is that there are few guarantees in business.

What can you do without guarantees? All you need to do. Get your plan, work it hard, work it smart, work it with people who can help you reach your goals, and work it Solomon's way.

And take some well-placed tips from a former mobster.

GET THE MESSAGE

1. Machiavelli says that businesses operate as if anything goes as long as you achieve your goals. Solomon says honesty, integrity, and hard work are the cornerstones of a successful business model. Which philosophy do you want your business to operate under?

2. There is no one secret that explains the success of a wealthy person's business interests, but successful businesses work within a framework. Solomon offers a solid structure and some brilliant principles upon which you can work to build your company's success.

CHAPTER FIVE

Lead with Your Brain, Not Your Mouth

It was the summer of 1979. Dad had been recently paroled from prison. He and I would spend our early mornings together sipping coffee and downing a bagel in the kitchen of his home in Roslyn, Long Island. I had been a soldier in the family for the better part of four years. It was during these early morning encounters that dad would school me further on the intricacies of the mob life, giving me the benefit of his thirty-odd years of membership in the underworld. For me, it was like going to college. I was attending the University of La Cosa Nostra. Dad was the wily old professor. I was the bright-eyed student, eager to absorb all the knowledge he was willing to share.

During these morning sessions I rarely spoke. I listened to how he navigated the choppy waters of our secret life. And I learned a lot during those sessions. Some of it was basic mob stuff. Some was really eye-opening.

Dad employed dramatic tactics when he wanted to make a point, like he used to do when I was a kid. He would make up stories about the horrors of addicts to emphasize how dangerous it was to abuse drugs. When I told him I wanted to buy a motorcycle, he spun stories about guys he knew who got killed on their bikes. I believed him. He made quite an impression. To this day, I have never smoked weed or owned a motorcycle.

During one session, dad motioned for me to leave the table and follow him as he walked into the bathroom. Dad turned on both faucets full blast and flushed the toilet. He then bowed his head toward the streaming water and motioned for me to do the same. "Your mouth will get you in trouble quicker than a gun or a knife," he told me. "Your words can be a greater weapon against you than anything the feds can drum up." His conclusion: "Know when to keep your mouth shut!"

A fool's lips bring him strife, and his mouth invites a beating.

SOLOMON

Dad was trying to show me that in our life we never knew who might be wearing a wire or whether or not there was a tap on the phone or a bug in the car, under the table, or in the wall of the room we were meeting in. Dad placed a premium on controlling one's mouth. Because of him, so did I. Not true about some of the guys in my crew. Let me tell you about Jerry Zimmerman.

Jerry and His Big, Fat Mouth

Jerry was a business associate who had a habit of doing—and saying—the wrong thing in almost any situation. He stood six foot, four inches tall and weighed a solid 270 pounds. He was a smooth talker who ran his mouth faster than a mobster pulling a hijacking. Scam artist, pure and simple. And he was darn good at it. He was groomed in the car business, and his salesmanship was legendary. One of the best.

I met the "big guy," as he was known in mob circles, during the days of Joe Colombo's ill-fated Italian American Civil Rights League. The late family boss created the league in 1970. It was a bluff. He wanted to show the world that there was no Mafia and that the FBI was persecuting Italian Americans. (As it turned out, the league did end the Mafia for my old boss, but not like he intended. It got him killed.) Jerry wasn't Italian. He was Jewish, but he had mob connections and was recruited to support the league's efforts. Mob guys might think Italians are superior, but they'll work with anyone. They don't have time for silly prejudices.

In 1977, two years after I was "straightened out" (mob lingo for getting made), I had the big guy manage an auto dealership I owned on Long Island. I was in the office one day when I overheard what sounded like an argument outside. My office was on the second floor and overlooked the lot. Sure enough, there was Jerry railing away with another guy. They were both waving their arms and jacking up the volume.

Then it was over. Jerry stormed into my office. I asked him about the commotion. He told me the story with a fire in his eyes. A customer was unhappy with a car he was sold and chose to express his dissatisfaction to the big guy, who didn't buy into his complaints.

"I couldn't believe this guy!" roared Jerry. "He demanded I give him a new car. Then he threatened me with some mob guy named Mario. I told him to get back in his car, pick up his spaghetti-bending goombah, and drive off the nearest cliff because he wasn't getting squat!"

"Jerry, I told you not to talk that way," I said. "Maybe he does have a friend, and you shouldn't be disrespectful like that."

"He doesn't know anyone. He's a mocky Jew blowhard just blowing off steam. Trust me, I know my own kind." So he thought.

Adventures in Saving Jerry's Life

A few days after Jerry's encounter I received a call from Tony, a soldier in my family, who said he needed to see me that evening on 18th Avenue in Bensonhurst. Mob meetings on 18th Avenue were usually held at the 19th Hole, a social club owned by powerful Lucchese family consigliere Christopher "Christie Tick" Furnari. I told Tony I would be there. Preferring not to drive myself, I told Jerry and another one of my guys, Vinny Aspromonte, that they would be driving me to Brooklyn that evening.

When we arrived, Tony was waiting outside. He told me another capo with the Genovese family wanted to see me and he was waiting in a different restaurant down the street. Since I had never met him, Tony would have to make the formal introduction. For security reasons, made men who didn't know each other had to be introduced by another made man who was familiar to both. After parking the car Jerry and Vinny joined us, and we walked a short distance to the restaurant. I told my guys to have a drink at the bar while Tony and I met the capo in a back room.

We entered and found the rotund Genovese capo sitting with another soldier at a big, round table. They stood up to greet us, and Tony proceeded to make the formal introduction. "Michael, *amico nostro*, Mario. Mario is a caporegime with the Genoveses." If you guessed *amico nostro* means "a friend of ours," you're catching on. It's code used to introduce made men to one another, verifying their formal membership in La Cosa Nostra. We all sat down. An angry Mario fired the first question.

"Do you know a Jew named Jerry Zimmerman?" It hit me like a ton of bricks. This was *the car lot* Mario. The one that Jerry was certain didn't exist.

"I know Jerry," I calmly responded. "He's with me."

Without blinking, Mario shot back. "I want him dead!" He was pounding the table with his fist. "He disrespected me to my brother-in-law, and I want him dead." (Houston, we have another problem!)

That was Machiavelli talking: "[T]he injury that is to be done to a man, ought to be of such a kind that one does not stand in fear of revenge." Back to what started it all, Jerry should have listened to Solomon: "He who guards his lips guards his life, but he who speaks rashly will come to ruin."

Jerry's messy encounter was lousy business. Common sense and restraint would have been the better tactic. Flying off the handle with a customer or client won't normally prove fatal to one's life, but it might prove fatal to one's business in the long run. Taking the high road with an unruly customer and employing a diplomatic approach to resolving an issue should be the strategy used whenever possible. You never know who you're dealing with. Take it figuratively or not, but they just might have a relative named Mario.

If the angry capo knew the big guy was in the restaurant there would be trouble—and maybe blood. I needed to get him out of the place, and fast. I excused myself, said I had to use the restroom after the long drive from Long Island. I went straight to the bar and told Jerry to drop his drink and get his butt out of the restaurant. "Mario is in the back room, and he's not happy," I said. "There's a diner down the street. I'll meet you there when I'm done." (We had no cell phones then.) I then rejoined the sit-down.

I could have put the discussion off, demanding my caporegime be present, but I decided to hear what Mario had to say, which was plenty. Zimmerman disrespected his brother-in-law, Mario fumed, especially when he called him a "spaghetti-bending goombah." I knew the rules. There was no toleration for disrespecting a made man. Consequences were severe. The situation was complicated. I was at a severe disadvantage. This guy was an old-time caporegime, and I was just a young soldier. If he demanded Jerry's head, I was supposed to serve it up. But this is where it gets tricky. I wasn't going to do it.

I told the aging capo that Jerry had been around me and the Colombo family for a long time. "No way would he ever be disrespectful to you or any other *friend of ours*," I lied. "He knows better." Mario argued that his brother-in-law would not lie, and because he was family, his word carried more weight. I disagreed. He then said he wanted them both at the table and he would prove his brother-in-law was telling the truth. That wouldn't work. I already knew Jerry had a problem controlling his tongue. I also already knew if Mario baited him into even the slightest admission of any disrespect, his fate would be sealed. *Finito.* "Not necessary," I said. "I was there during the encounter. I overheard the argument from my office, and Jerry never disrespected you," I lied once again. I knew my word had to be accepted above a sucker's, regardless of whether he was family or not. He wasn't made, and a sucker's word was never to be taken over that of a made man's. Mario insisted his brother-in-law would not lie, that I might have missed that exchange, and that he was within his rights to kill the disrespectful Jew. I insisted that it was his brother-in-law who was lying in an effort to get himself a new car. I also said that if anything were to happen to Jerry, his brother-in-law would meet the same fate.

It went on for almost an hour. Neither one of us gave an inch. Those old-timers took the *respect* issue way too seriously. I had to end this matter before it went to the next level. Mario was so steamed, I worried a future sit-down with my capo might result in a decision to appease Mario. I didn't want to risk my capo making a politically correct decision to have my guy put in a hospital for a few weeks. A *tactical retreat* was the only way I was going to break the standoff between us and save Jerry from bodily harm, temporary or permanent.

> If you do nothing in a difficult time, your strength is limited.
> Rescue those being taken off to death, and save those stumbling toward slaughter.
>
> SOLOMON

Sometimes it is better to accept less in a negotiation than to walk away a total loser, especially when a total loss could have a

major impact on your business. A tactical retreat is tantamount
to a compromise and will almost always prove better than defeat.
In my negotiation with Mario, I quickly realized that my goal
was to keep the big guy breathing. I was unwilling to accept anything less. I also realized I wasn't going to win the argument
unless I was willing to give up something in return. There were
many times during my business negotiations with lenders, suppliers, and partners when a compromise was the only solution.
When both sides emerge satisfied, everybody wins. Unless you
are holding all the cards, it is not smart to be rigid.

Mario wanted to come out a winner for his brother-in-law,
so I offered a solution that would accomplish just that. I would
give his brother-in-law a new car, and I would sternly admon-
ish Jerry for being disrespectful to his sister's husband. He
would be a hero to his guy, and Jerry would continue to breathe.
Maybe I would take the cost of the car out of his bonus. Mario
sniffed the bait but said the big guy still needed some pain. Not
acceptable, I said. After another fifteen minutes of ego strok-
ing, I set the hook. Mario accepted the offer. Jerry would see the
dawn. But I sure gave him an earful on the drive home.

Jerry Goes to Hollywood

Jerry had a brother in the car business in Los Angeles. I recom-
mended a visit for a few months. Mario might reconsider. No
need to say it twice. Jerry was packed and headed west within a
week.

Jerry wasted no time in waging an assault on Hollywood. I
should have realized his close proximity to the glamour of

Tinsel Town would be too hard to resist. Then I got the call: "I'm getting into the movie business," he said. "I have a script and a director for a horror movie titled *Mausoleum*, and I want you to be my partner." I didn't need a crystal ball to tell me what was coming next. "The budget is $250,000. I need you to put up a third."

I asked him what he knew about making movies. He went on to tell me how easy it was and how much I would enjoy visiting the set and being involved in the production. He would even grace me with the title of executive producer, whatever that meant. I figured the $83,000 he was asking me for would spare me the trouble of saving him from whomever it was he would beat for the money if I refused to invest. Besides, despite all of his crazy antics, I had a soft spot for the big guy. He kept me amused with his endless adventures.

"I'll send you the money," I told him. "You had better make this work."

"Piece of cake," said Jerry, "I was born for this business." Maybe. But not for finance. The film started over budget, and that wasn't the half of it.

Just a few weeks in, I get a call. A guy named Jack Gilardi wants to speak to me.

Gilardi was a talent agent with International Creative Management or ICM, one of the biggest and most influential firms in the industry. Gilardi said he has something important to discuss and wanted to know when I'd be in the neighborhood. Jerry!

I had Jerry pick me up at the airport on the day of the meeting. As we drove to the hotel, I asked him about Gilardi. Jerry kicked off a defensive, fast-talking, profanity-laced diatribe. Gilardi and ICM were taking advantage, he said. Gilardi had provided the talent for the movie and was now asking for the customary 10 percent the agency charged.

Jerry ran off a litany of reasons why the agency was not entitled to its fee. Everything but the kitchen sink. "You're gonna back me up on this one, chief, aren't you?" I had already invested $500,000 in a movie Zimmerman originally budgeted at half that. If ICM was getting a check, it would be drawn on Jerry's account, and there was nothing Jerry hated more than reaching into his pocket. For a guy who stood so tall, he had the shortest arms I ever saw.

My first impulse was to stand behind Jerry as I'd done at the car dealership. But something told me I should hear what Gilardi had to say. Gilardi wasn't a wiseguy, and ICM wasn't a mob family. Jerry's rear end wasn't at risk—just his ego and bank balance. "Let's get to the meeting," I said.

Hollywood agents are notorious for arriving late to meetings, especially those who boast an impressive client roster. When we arrived, Gilardi was already there waiting for us. Impressive.

We walked over. He rose to greet us. He was impeccably dressed. Dark suit and tie. Something in his appearance and mannerisms told me that L.A. was not his hometown. We sat, ordered drinks, and exchanged small talk about Los Angeles traffic, the weather, and the movie business. I took a liking to him. Gilardi told me he was originally from Chicago, one of my favorite cities. Then it was business time.

Why the meeting? Before Gilardi could answer, Jerry blurted out an embarrassing opening statement. Classic Zimmerman. He always led with his mouth. Out came the laundry list of reasons ICM shouldn't get its fee. The talent was no good. ICM didn't provide the talent they requested. The talent caused him to go over budget. He even suggested I look to ICM to recoup some of the money I invested in the overblown production.

Gilardi and I listened. He went on for a good five minutes, blaming everything but the death of Marilyn Monroe on the evil ICM. Jerry finally ran out of breath and Gilardi sat there stunned. He didn't quite know how to respond to Jerry's ranting. I spared him the trouble.

Listen and Think—Then Speak
If You Absolutely Must

Regardless of how many times I had admonished the big guy to hold his tongue, he just could not restrain himself. He was constantly getting himself into business disputes with others that resulted in a sit-down. In most cases he was the one at fault. But he was my guy. I was always there to defend him. That didn't stop him from making it difficult by always shooting off his mouth before he heard what the other party had to say. In doing so, he usually buried himself before the other guy had even lifted a shovel. This time was no different.

> He who answers before listening—that is his folly and his shame.
>
> SOLOMON

I cannot stress enough the importance of becoming a good listener in your dealings. It conditions you to gather information before acting or making a decision that will impact your business. It puts you in the habit of looking before you leap. You learn to make informed decisions, based upon your research and the information you acquired about the particular situation you are dealing with. A person's business instincts are much sharper when those instincts have been nourished with information and honed to a fine point through experience. The big guy just never got it. And he was about to suffer the consequences for it.

I asked Jerry a few simple questions. I said I only wanted yes or no answers. "Did ICM provide the talent for the film?" "Yes," he responded. "Did the talent actually work in the film?" "Yes," he said again. "Was there an agreement between ICM and your production company that provided for ICM to be paid a fee for the talent they provided?" "Yes," he answered, a bit more sheepishly this time. "Did you, in fact pay ICM the money you had agreed to pay?" Having reached his limit of affirmative answers, Jerry started ranting about some crazy incident that allegedly occurred the day Annette Funicello visited the set.

Whoa! Annette Funicello? What did she have to do with it? Gilardi then explained that he was married to Annette, and she accompanied him to the set on the day Jerry was blabbing about. "You're married to Annette Funicello? Mouseketeer Annette?"

It was over for Jerry. You gotta understand, almost every boy growing up in the 1950s who watched *The Mickey Mouse Club* was in love with Mouseketeer Annette. I was no exception. I mean, before wanting to become a made man in the notorious Colombo crime family, I wanted to be a Mouseketeer just so I could be in the club with Annette. Now here I was at a sit-down, representing one of my guys who was trying to beat the husband of my childhood sweetheart out of his rightfully earned money. I never would have known this if Jerry hadn't yammered on. No reason for Gilardi to mention his wife in the context of the business at hand. How would he know I had a soft spot for her? Jerry's argument was near dead on arrival. Now it was buried.

I let him finish the tirade before asking Gilardi how much his agency was owed. The figure was somewhere north of $20,000, if memory serves. I turned to my associate with a look that invited no retort. "Pay the man!"

Don't Think with Your Tongue

Before the big man could complain, I asked him if he intended to continue making movies. It didn't take a genius to figure out what his answer would be. He made one movie, a horror movie that didn't scare anyone but the investors, yet he thought he was on his way to being the next Alfred Hitchcock. Jerry was bitten by the movie bug.

"Why the heck would you want to beat a major talent agency out of their money?" I asked. "When they pass the word that you're a deadbeat to all the other agencies, you'll never get another actor to appear in your films." I admonished him to use his oversized brain in the future and to extend those short arms into his deep pockets and get ICM paid in a hurry. Case closed.

It worked out well for everyone. Jerry and I went on to produce and distribute a string of moderately successful B movies together, including *Knights of the City*, which worked out well for me. I met my future wife on the set of that film.

Gilardi and I have been close for more than thirty years, and he has very capably represented me in various film and television projects.

> The wise in heart accept commands, but a chattering fool comes to ruin.
>
>   SOLOMON

Solomon understood the folly of those who insisted on leading with their mouths instead of their brains. The most intelligent businesspeople I know are men and women of few, but very insightful and intelligent words. If you want to gain an advantage in life and achieve meaningful success in business, remember to look before you leap, learn before you speak, and never put your mouth before your brain.

GET THE MESSAGE

1. Your words can be a greater weapon against you than a gun or a knife. Know when to keep your mouth shut!

2. Take the high road with an unruly customer and employ a diplomatic approach to resolving an issue whenever possible. You never know who you're dealing with.

3. Unless you're holding all the cards, sometimes it's better to accept less in a negotiation than to walk away a total loser—especially when a total loss could have a major impact on your business. A tactical retreat will almost always prove better than defeat.

4. Become a good listener in your business dealings. It conditions you to

gather information before acting or making a decision that will impact your business. Your instincts will be much sharper when they are nourished with information and honed to a fine point through experience.

5. Look before you leap; learn before you speak; and never put your mouth before your brain.

CHAPTER SIX

Master the Art of the Sit-Down

Norby Walters, self-proclaimed "agent to the stars," was about to get his bell rung—mob-style. Norby had a multi-million-dollar business. That's normally a good thing. But he was holding out on the Colombo family brass. That's bad.

My dear old dad, Sonny Franzese, was Norby's undercompensated, silent partner. Dad didn't like being a victim, especially when it involved money. Sonny always got what was coming to him, and Norby was about to find out what happened when he didn't.

Negotiating . . . for His Life

Dad had me arrange an official meeting, in mob parlance a *sit-down*. This was not an invitation for Norby to join us for a bottle of Pinot Grigio and some calamari. The sit-down is fundamental to La Cosa Nostra culture. It is the single most important method used to discuss and resolve any issue.

The venue depends on the participants and subject matter. Since Norby wasn't a made man, and the issue involved a somewhat legitimate business deal, there was no reason to seek out a secure or secret venue. We met at the famous Stage Delicatessen on Seventh Avenue in Manhattan's Theatre District.

I remember the day exactly. It was summer. The place was packed—tables jammed together so tight, I could smell the pastrami breath of the guy sitting at the next table. The usual Stage crowd sat, chewed, and chattered. Other than the tourists, most were talking business. Execs, music-industry moguls, talent agents, lawyers, and celebrities negotiated contracts, planned their next tour or Broadway appearance, or chose songs for their upcoming record. You get the picture: "Will the 16 percent royalty work for your next album, Mr. Manilow?" And, "How about a role in a Broadway musical, Ms. Warwick?" And, "Should we give the new guy the Macy's account?" And, "Would you like to keep your brains in your head or on a slice of rye bread, Mr. Walters?" Mob business, entertainment business, corporate business. It was all the same. We were all there having some form of a sit-down. But the stakes were pretty high in Norby's case. He was negotiating for his life.

Pay the One You're "With"

Norby rose to prominence in the entertainment industry by managing and booking superstar recording acts. People like Rick James, Janet Jackson, Dionne Warwick, Lionel Ritchie, the Commodores, the Spinners, the Four Tops, Cameo, Miles Davis, Luther Vandross, Patti LaBelle, Kool & the Gang, New Edition, Ben Vereen, and Marvin Gaye. Norby was Jewish by birth but black by volition. He could slap hands, turn on the jive, and communicate with his clients as if he'd been raised in the hood, a major reason for his furiously growing client roster. He was making millions.

More than jive, Norby had muscle: My dad. To explain the relationship in mob vernacular, Norby Walters was "with" Sonny Franzese. When a businessman is "with" someone, it means he has a godfather, a gladiator who will protect him from anyone looking to move in on his business and into his pocket. Norby was Sonny's guy, an associate of the Colombo family, and that status made him "hands off" to anyone on the street. For this backup, Norby passed on a piece of the action to the Colombo family. Except Norby apparently forgot the mailing address. While my father was in the joint, Norby got out of the habit of paying.

When Dad got paroled, he wanted an accounting. "What's mine is mine," he said. "You don't let a sucker get into your pocket."

A *sucker* is anyone who is not made. Anyone. It doesn't matter if he is a longtime friend, a CEO, a superstar athlete, or the president of the United States. If you're not made, you're a sucker, and a sucker is never permitted to take advantage of a made man, especially when it comes to money. Dad wanted his cut. Every penny!

"Arrange a sit-down," Dad told me. "I'm going to handle this personally." I knew what that meant.

I really didn't want Norby to get whacked. I liked him. He amused me. I even considered him a friend. That's why I didn't lean on him to pay up while Dad was in the pen. That, and I had other business interests. I was raking in millions myself at the time.

More important, I didn't want Dad have his parole violated and returned to prison. My real concern here was an extortion charge. Gaetano "Corky" Vastola, a caporegime in the DeCavalcante family, put the muscle on a small-time record distributor from Philly and ended up with a stretch for extortion. His partner, Morris Levy, a legendary music mogul, died in jail awaiting appeal for the same beef. Extortion is a common charge for mobsters and their associates. Norby may have been with my dad for decades, but he was still a sucker. If Dad scared him, he might run to the feds.

I calmed Sonny down a bit. I convinced him to forget about whatever additional money was due for the past. Now that he was home, we would start fresh. I would make sure Dad got his end of the profits every week and the family would get theirs. Norby's business was booming, and the family would reap the benefits. The sit-down would be a lunch among old friends and business partners, forgetting the past and keeping an eye on the future. Except Norby's memory kept failing.

After exchanging pleasantries, ordering our sandwiches, and telling a few stories, Dad laid down the law. From that day forward, as an equal partner, he would be receiving his share of the profits on a weekly basis. Norby looked incredulous. What—he suddenly got amnesia? He didn't recall Sonny ever being a partner in the business. Dad was his man, sure, and he would gladly pay for the service he received as an associate of the Colombo family, but a *partner* in the business?

I saw the look in Sonny's eyes. It wasn't pretty. Slowly and deliberately, Dad pushed aside his sandwich. Lunch was over. The sit-down had begun.

My father reminded Norby of their history, how the

partnership started, walked him through every step and event. He could have delivered the message with footnotes and sworn testimony, for all the good it would do Norby's rotten memory.

"I don't recall agreeing to a partnership, Sonny," said Norby. "You know how much I respect you and how much I value our friendship, but I do not believe we are partners in the business. Besides, the margin of profit isn't great enough to support a partnership. It's all I can do to feed myself." Norby was lying through his teeth about that. We all knew what he was turning each month.

Sonny was rabid. Maybe the Stage was a bad idea after all. He was on the brink of reaching across the table and crushing Norby's larynx. Dad's temper was legendary, and it was never a good idea to get on his bad side. According to unsubstantiated FBI reports, more than thirty men from the streets had learned that the hard way.

"If I put a gun in your mouth and blow your brains out, would that refresh your memory?" Dad said. He didn't make idle threats. He was dead serious, and Norby knew it. His mouth dropped, and his face turned white.

People were starting to notice us now. I had to break the tension before it got ugly. It was time for me to start negotiating what was on the agenda for this sit-down—saving Norby's life. While looking Norby dead in the eye, I told my father there must be a misunderstanding. "Isn't that right, Norby?" On cue, dumbstruck Norby slowly nodded his head in agreement. I told Dad that I would get with Norby later and work out the arrangement between them.

I then changed course and reminded Norby that he and I had planned to produce a number of movies and concerts together, and that there would be enough for everyone to get their share. Norby nodded his head again—this time more vigorously—as he regained his ability to speak.

Dad's expression began to lighten up, just barely. Norby's color started coming back. He saw that my proposal was beginning to appease Dad. As Norby's advocate, I would resolve the immediate issue, save the agent's life, and work out the deal points in friendlier confines later. After explaining to Dad how much potential upside we were looking at, the dark mood lifted. After a little more small talk, a cup of coffee, and a piece of cheesecake, the sit-down was over. Norby could not get out the door fast enough.

Whether or not my father was Norby's legitimate partner was not the issue. The issue was money. Had Norby been smart, he would have given the family its cut, and he would have avoided a near-death experience. The business could afford it even if his pride couldn't. The most important part of a sit-down is getting clarity on an issue, cutting to the chase, and reaching resolution.

The Nature of the Sit-Down

Much of what I learned in business I learned from sit-downs. Thinking on my feet, building my case, knowing the parties involved—and how to pull their levers. It was all part of the routine. And the routine was constant. You've seen *Donnie Brasco*? Remember the scene when he explains how mobsters use *fuggedaboutit*? It's the same with the sit-down. It's universal and multifunctional.

"Did that mamaluke pay his vig? We gotta sit down." "Who we taking in the game tonight? We gotta sit down." "We gonna break this bum's legs! We gotta sit down." "Where we gonna eat tonight? We gotta sit down." You get the picture. The sit-down is so ingrained in a made guy's vocabulary, it caused one FBI agent listening in on a secretly installed bug to remark, "Do these guys ever decide anything standing up?"

A sit-down is also La Cosa Nostra's version of a high-stakes negotiation at the corporate bargaining table. The meetings normally take place in the back rooms of mob social clubs or in the basement of a member's house to avoid getting noticed by the cops. In my day, there were no fancy conference rooms with expensive leather chairs or high-powered technology. And there definitely was no assistant taking down minutes or flipping through PowerPoint slides. Black coffee with anisette or stregga would be served to the participants by a trusted associate, who would then excuse himself from the room only to return if summoned. After a few brief formalities, such as introducing members who might not have previously met, the negotiations would begin.

Although the locations for sit-downs are a far cry from the often overstated conference rooms of the corporate world, the matters discussed are not. At sit-downs mob executives negotiate deals concerning hundreds of millions of dollars, prevent or advance the hostile takeover of a company or labor union, or decide the fate of a dishonest employee. Virtually every matter concerning the business of organized crime is hashed out, negotiated, and decided at a sit-down.

The more diverse and extensive a member's interests are, the more often he will be a participant at the mob's negotiating table. As my business empire continued to expand and prosper, it was rare that a day went by when I was not sitting across the table from another soldier, capo or boss, either from my own family or another, negotiating any one of a number of issues. A made man will never achieve success in the business world of organized crime if he does not master the "art of the sit-down." And make no mistake; there is an art to achieving success at such meetings.

The Chicken Caper

Right before I was inducted into the family, I hit the street with a vengeance, determined to make the money needed to help spring my dad. The early successes I enjoyed in my various business ventures prior to the life did not go unnoticed by the guys in the pinstriped suits. As word of my financial prowess spread through the cafés and social clubs of Brooklyn, along came the wiseguys, including a gang of prison-fresh entrepreneurs directed to me by my father.

Jimmy Testa was said to be a wizard at the fruit-and-veggie business. My father sent the newly paroled con to me with a ringing endorsement. He came with a proposition that resulted in my fronting him $25,000 (1970s dollars) to open a market in Suffolk County, Long Island. We called it Sonny's Farm Circle, in honor of my dear old dad. Within the market was a butcher shop. Homemade Italian sausages, bracciola, and the best cuts of meats were proudly displayed in sparkling clean refrigerated showcases. Only the best-quality meats were marketed, including A-1 homegrown chickens.

Or so I thought.

One sunny afternoon, a very nice woman placed an order for a few hundred pounds of chicken to be the main course at her family's annual Memorial Day barbecue. The chickens were delivered and paid for by this most appreciative customer. On the Tuesday following the holiday weekend, however, the adoring woman returned to the market with a bad attitude and a trunk full of rotting chickens. Apparently, it was maggots and not her weekend revelers that got to feast on the birds. That's right—maggots! The grade A hens were infested with them.

After removing the decaying poultry from the woman's car, we immediately gave her a full refund to cover the cost of the chickens. That didn't quite make up for her aborted weekend barbecue. After she adamantly refused an offer for a fresh batch of hens, we loaded her up with all sorts of market goodies in an attempt to keep her chicken experience under wraps. Realizing that a maggot-filled-chicken story could spell death for a neighborhood market, we went well out of our way to soften her memory of a backyard full of barbecue-deprived guests. Apparently, that mission was accomplished as she left assuring us we had not lost her as a customer. It was now time to deal with the company who provided the infested birds. I was chomping at the bit.

Since the chickens were ordered specifically for the weekend barbecue and arrived at the market on the same day they were delivered to our customer, the market could not be held responsible for the invasion of the maggots. Normally, a situation like this would be resolved by the supplier reimbursing the market for the cost of the chickens, with a couple of pounds of free poultry thrown in as an act of contrition. But this was no ordinary chicken supplier. These chickens had a godfather, one who just happened to be the boss of the Gambino crime family, Paul Castellano. Earlier in his career, he launched a successful wholesale poultry distribution business that, at its height, supplied three hundred butchers in and around New York City. He also had two major supermarket chains, Key Foods and Waldbaums under his thumb.

Although I had not yet taken the oath, I was an official recruit and was required to put my business ventures on record with the family, the market included. As a courtesy to Big Paul, I was asked by my caporegime, Andrew Russo, to buy the market's meats from his company, and that included—you guessed it—the chickens. In other words, *he made me an offer I couldn't refuse.* There would be no violation of antitrust laws here. No competitive bids—or birds, in my case—would be submitted. Big Paul had a clear cut monopoly among the city's five families.

While Big Paul was minding the Gambino family, a relative by the name of Peter Castellano (believed to be his younger brother) was minding the henhouse. I placed a call to Peter and explained the issue, assuming he would offer to credit the market for the decayed birds. His response was Machiavellian swift. He told me to eat the chickens, maggots and all; that he had delivered them in edible order; and that he fully expected to collect the money due for the now putrefied poultry. Not the response I anticipated.

I respectfully replied that he had as much chance of collecting payment for the birds as the birds had in making it to the barbecue. And furthermore, he could take his rotting chicken business elsewhere, as he would no longer be my supplier. The conversation then proceeded to get heated. Actually, it got downright ugly. After a few choice salutations were exchanged, the call ended with the handsets being slammed down. This was not yet the era of the cell phone. Realizing that I had just gotten into it with Big Paul's blood relative, I thought it best to make the drive to Brooklyn and put the incident on record with my caporegime.

Monte's restaurant on Carroll Street was the unofficial Colombo family headquarters. When I arrived there that evening, I was greeted by both my caporegime (who was also the acting family underboss) and the family boss himself, Tom Dibella. Apparently, word of the infamous "chicken caper" had already been hatched. Big Paul had reached out to my boss, and from the looks I received from the Colombo brass, he was not happy. For the next half hour I was grilled about the incident by my superiors. They were told I was disrespectful to Peter, who was not only a made man but a relative of the Gambino family. I was only a recruit. Who the heck did I think I was? To say they were angry was an understatement.

Now, one might be thinking this is really not that big a deal. We are only talking about a few hundred dollars' worth of chickens. But these were mob chickens, and this was mob business. The issue now became a matter of respect. Let me give you a sense of the danger here: Paul Castellano allegedly had his daughter's boyfriend whacked because the kid poked fun at Big Paul's appearance. He compared Big Paul to poultry magnate Frank Perdue and said he looked like one of the plucked birds he peddled all over the city. He was right. But he still ended up dead, and now the powerful Gambino family boss believed I had disrespected his handpicked relative, which was tantamount to disrespecting him. And I was merely a lowly recruit still trying to earn my stripes. Are you getting the picture? Houston, we have a problem! A super-sized one.

After respectfully absorbing a brow beating from my two superiors, I was finally given the opportunity to relay my version of the incident. Isn't it amazing how stories can vary so dramatically depending on who is providing the narrative? That is especially true when mobsters are telling the stories. When I was finished, I got nothing but a cold, hard stare from each of my bosses. The table was engulfed in a dead silence for what seemed an eternity, but in reality was only a few seconds. Then, as if on cue, both bosses erupted in a good, hearty belly laugh. I mean, they were hysterical! The maggot-filled chickens were too much for them to take seriously.

Apparently, I wasn't the only guy who'd had a chicken incident with Big Paul. His chicken mishaps were legendary in mob land. Much to my relief, both men began rattling off chicken jokes, while tossing a dig or two toward Big Paul himself. It was all in the family now. We were Colombo guys enjoying a little revelry at the expense of another family's boss. It appeared I would get a pass on this one. My bosses would back me up. Big Paul would not have me sleeping with the chickens. No harm, no fowl (pardon the pun), at least until the sit-down that would no doubt be convened. It would be the first of many I would attend during my life in La Cosa Nostra.

In preparation for the sit-down, I was given the following orders by my bosses:

- Be respectful at all times to both Big Paul and Peter.
- Remain quiet at all times unless I was told by one of my bosses to speak.

- Be firm and definite in response to their questions.
- Do not respond to either Big Paul's or Peter's questions.
- Do not call either a liar regardless of how blatant the lie is they are telling.
- Do not respond to any derogatory remarks thrown at me from either of the chicken mavens.
- Without question do not admit to being disrespectful to Peter in any way during the infamous chicken telephone call (even though I had uttered a few choice words in response to his), as any admission in that regard might prove hazardous to my health.
- Accept without comment whatever decision is reached at the table regarding the disposition of the chicken caper.

Finally, I was reminded that I was only a recruit, sitting at a table full of made men, accused of being insubordinate and disrespectful not only to a made man, but to the made relative of the boss. And adding insult to injury, I was refusing to pay the Gambino family boss money he claimed was due him. To put it bluntly, I was still in deep trouble. Although I was assured my bosses would go to the mat for me, if I were to make a mistake at the table, become insubordinate, or admit to being disrespectful to Peter, I would lose my argument and would suffer the consequences that would inevitably follow.

When the sit-down was finally convened, Big Paul pounced on me from the start, admonishing me for being disrespectful to his man and in turn to him. Peter then took his turn relaying the phone conversation that I certainly didn't recall having. There must have been static on the line. The chicken mavens continued to hammer me throughout, trying to bait me into an admission of guilt or an insubordinate remark. In spite of the maven's verbal onslaught, I calmly followed the script as I was ordered to do.

DiBella and Russo would effectively present my version of the incident, and in the end the brothers would reluctantly agree to a decision in my favor. Peter was ordered to eat the cost of the rotten fowls—figuratively, not literally—and we were both ordered to continue doing business as before, minus the decaying birds, of course. I would remain on my guard, however, realizing that the powerful duo reluctantly agreed to the outcome and that I would not be on their preferred customer list from this point on. Mobsters have long memories when they think they've been screwed.

More Sit-Downs, Fewer Meetings

I have attended a number of sit-downs along with my fair share of business meetings. One thing is certain: a sit-down is a heck of a lot more efficient at resolving matters and getting things accomplished than a corporate board meeting.

Be honest; how often have you been asked to attend an important company meeting only to spend two hours sitting around a table wondering why on earth the meeting was scheduled to begin with? In that span of time, the supposed agenda is never made clear, different voices are clamoring for attention, ideas get rerouted to pointless conversations, and when the talking heads finally stop putting in their two cents, trying to make themselves look important, you rush out the door and spend the remainder of the day responding to e-mails and phone calls that have piled up during the wasted two hours.

That never happens at a sit-down. Never has and never will. Unless they're clueless, everyone knows exactly why they are there. The agenda is made crystal clear. "Do we whack him, or not?" The participants come prepared, and they suffer the consequences if they don't. Few words are wasted. Rest assured, a resolution will be reached.

This is a model of efficiency everyone in business should follow. Aside from the threats of physical violence and the extreme psychological torture, corporate America would be a lot more productive if it eliminated the "business meeting" and replaced it with the sit-down.

Learning to be an effective negotiator was not the only skill I acquired from the countless sit-downs I participated in during my years as a made man. The years I spent sitting down with some of the most powerful organized crime figures in the country, my contemporaries at the time, provided me with a wealth of information that proved valuable in both business and in life.

> Wisdom is supreme; therefore get wisdom. Though it cost you all you have, get understanding.
>
> SOLOMON

Mastering the art of the sit-down prepared me for meetings I entered into with real estate developers, executives in the movie business, union presidents, oil barons, high-powered bankers, and attorneys from the United States Department of Justice.

There can be no better preparation for mastering one's

negotiating skills than to have participated in and mastered the art of the sit-down. I approached every business meeting and negotiation as if it were a sit-down. The skills I employed gave me a distinct edge in almost every case and allowed me to earn millions of dollars. Regular attendance should be a prerequisite for anyone aspiring to obtain a degree in business. However, since that is a virtual impossibility for anyone who has not taken a blood oath and dedicated his life to La Cosa Nostra, allow someone who has to provide you with some inside information. Master the following skills and at *your next sit-down* you will have your business associates doing all but kissing your ring.

> Do not forsake wisdom, and she will protect you; love her,
> and she will watch over you.
>
> SOLOMON

5 Steps to Mastering the Sit-Down

1. Enter with both gun barrels loaded. If a mob guy engages in a sit-down either inexperienced or unprepared, he will literally be eaten up by the mob executives who have surely mastered the techniques of their trade. His position in the negotiation can have the strongest argument at the table, but if he doesn't know how to play the internal dynamics, he'll be left standing with his pants down and his pockets empty. If he falls into a trap the more experienced participants will inevitably set in the negotiation, he will end up a loser and will not be given the opportunity to renegotiate his position—at least not at the current sit-down.

All decisions are binding. The only thing more final than the decision is disregarding it. Preparation is vital to a mob guy's success, his livelihood, and sometimes his life.

Because of my experience with sit-downs, prepping for business meetings or negotiations is second nature. In either case the basics are the same:

- Know my position and be prepared to capably present and defend it with materials and evidence.
- Know the temperament of the people with whom I am meeting. Are they fair or treacherous, even-tempered or bloodthirsty? This helps in adapting my negotiation tactics to the situation.
- Have some knowledge of the company the parties are involved with, if any. I do my homework. I find out who is on the board of executives. I find out how much revenue they pulled in last year. I find out why their stocks went down in the last six months.

It's not brain surgery I'm teaching here and I'm sure you have heard this before. People with type A personalities prepare for meetings because they are meticulous and pay close attention to details. Mob guys prepare for sit-downs because they like to keep their money in their pockets and their knees in the proper place. Beneath both motivations, there is a more basic motivation—one that everyone can understand. You prepare for a meeting because you want to give yourself the best opportunity to succeed in achieving your goals. Coming *in* with both barrels loaded means having a better chance of coming *out* a winner.

2. Lead with your brain, not your mouth. The smart mob guys, the ones who survived long enough to get maximum use of their mouths, are those who know how to keep their traps shut. In a sit-down, I always found it valuable to let the other guy talk. Even when I had to make the opening statement, I made it short, sweet, and to the point. I won many arguments by letting my adversary in the sit-down run his mouth and eventually make a mistake I could capitalize on.

In a business sit-down, I always find it valuable to let the other person talk more, especially if I don't know much about him before entering the meeting. By letting the other person babble, I often learn what to say and what not to say. How to position a detail or why I should not mention something or other.

You can learn a lot by listening. More so if the other guy's a yapper. We have all been in meetings with the guy who asks a question and answers it before you have a chance to respond. "A fool is known by his many words." And so is his position. That's what Solomon said, and as the king, he was in sit-downs all the time—foreign dignitaries, trade emissaries, ambassadors, military commanders, local governors, and magistrates. I have never seen a person with that problem achieve meaningful success, and I have been around my share of blowhards. They manage to talk themselves out of accomplishing something and never seem to know why.

At your next sit-down, talk enough to accomplish what you need. Just don't talk too much, especially in today's business culture, where nobody has the time or the patience for meaningless chatter. In a sit-down silence is not only golden; it's smart.

3. Check your ego at the door. Oh, the joy of being under-estimated. I was one of the younger mobsters, so the old-timers always believed they were schooling me. At sit-downs, I would purposely ask the old warhorses questions that I knew the answer to just to have them believe they were smarter than me. I would do that right up front to disarm them for the battle ahead and get them believing I was no match for them at the table. Then, when the games began, I'd catch them off guard and move in for the proverbial kill.

It's a great tactic, especially when the person you are meeting with has an inflated ego. Gambino boss John Gotti could never keep his ego in check. Neither could Colombo capo Charles "Charlie Moose" Panarella or Genovese family capo Collie Di Pietro. I sat down with all of them, and their egos could fill the whole venue. Each thought he was the smartest person at the table, in the room, or in all of mob land for that matter. That was okay with me. As long as I got what I wanted at the sit-down, they could all believe they were the second coming of Niccolò Machiavelli for all I cared.

People with big mouths and bigger egos are easily identified. Should you encounter such a person at your next sit-down, let his or her weakness be your strength. I have employed that strategy many times in my business dealings when the situation called for it. Start out as the student, finish as the teacher, and leave with the spoils.

4. Never act like the weakest link—especially if you are. There were times when I knew I was outgunned at a sit-down. Face it, people: you are not always the smartest person in the room. But acting like you're outgunned to gain an advantage with your opponent is one thing. Actually being outgunned is quite another. At a mob sit-down, you're dead meat if you don't match up. No different in a business sit-down. So how do you appear to be the smarter person when you know you're not? The less you say, the more intelligent you sound.

> Even a fool is thought wise if he keeps silent, and discerning
> if he holds his tongue.
>
> SOLOMON

The words you don't say make you smart. A few well-placed comments here and there make you appear a lot smarter than you might be. Anytime I entered a meeting knowing my argument was a loser going in, I was able to gain a compromise by having my opponent believe I could hold my own. And as we would say on the street, "sometimes a half a loaf of bread is better than none at all."

5. Be Respectful. At a mob sit-down, disrespect of any kind is not tolerated. Voices are rarely raised, and insults are never hurled, regardless of how serious the issue at hand might be. This policy ensures that business remains business and doesn't get personal.

A violation of this policy is often met with extreme consequences for the offending party. Respect for one another is demanded, and personal differences are not allowed to stand in the way of resolving the issue under discussion. At sit-downs, mob guys stay focused on the issue and bring it to a conclusion. At a business sit-down, matters rarely get resolved when discussions get heated. The more contentious the meetings or negotiations get, the less productive they become. At your next sit-down, remember you're there to achieve a specific goal. Do not allow an emotional response to another person at the table to stand in the way of meeting it.

Don't Meet—Sit

If you want to make quick and effective decisions, I recommend you make every meeting you attend from now on a sit-down—it works with or without the corned beef sandwiches.

When I finished with Norby, I advised him to play it straight. "Do the right thing with the family. The next time I won't be able to save you." I now had leverage for him to ante up a healthy share of the profits to the family without my having to put the arm on a man I considered a friend. The family would get its money, and Norby would keep his life. All in all, it was a successful day.

GET THE MESSAGE

1. Eliminate the "business meeting" and replace it with the sit-down. Aside from the threats of physical violence and the extreme psychological torture, corporate America would be a lot more productive.

2. Don't come unprepared: Know your position; know the temperament of the people you are meeting with; and do your homework. Come in with both barrels loaded and you have a better chance of coming out a winner.

3. Don't let your ego rule. Pull back and let the other people do the talking. You can learn a lot by listening—especially if you don't know much about the person before entering the meeting—and letting the other person babble may help you learn what to say **and** what not to say.

4. Keep your cool. The more contentious the meetings or negotiations get, the less productive they become.

CHAPTER SEVEN

Keep Your Eyes on the Bookies

We live in a global gambling culture. Courtesy of the World Wide Web, access to a gambling experience is accessible within five minutes of almost anyone living in any developed nation in the world. In the United States, we have some form of legalized gambling in forty-eight of the fifty states. Whether it be the Internet, a casino, a card room, video poker, the ponies, a state-run lottery, or the mob's own bookmakers, opportunities to gamble are everywhere and available for the taking.

You better ask yourself a question: Does this easy access to the garden variety of gaming opportunities pose a threat to business? Stick with me to find out.

Stacking the Deck

Gambling has always been an effective tool of the street, as well as a valued source of income. When a businessman's gambling habits become obsessive—and let me tell you, that's quite often the case—it usually leads to additional revenue. for the mob's bookmakers. Sometimes it even leads to a newfound business acquisition for the family, if you know what I mean.

This book is about achieving and maintaining success in business, right? I would be negligent if I failed to warn you about the possible impact gambling can have on your business. (Besides, can a former mob guy write a book on business without dealing with the La Cosa Nostra's most lucrative and revered enterprise? Fuggedaboutit.) A gambling issue—whether your own, your partner's, an employee's, or even a stranger's on the street—can impact your business and your life in a big way. No one should want to see a business fail and a life be ruined because of gambling.

Most of my adult life I have dealt with people whose lives have been destroyed and whose enterprises were left in ruins over this problem. As a mobster enriching himself on the habits of gamblers, I helped destroy several businesses. I personally took ownership of a Chevrolet dealership on Long Island from a businessman who couldn't pay his debts (to the tune of several hundred thousand dollars). I watched as owners lost restaurants, athletes shaved points in games, bankers passed bad checks, casino managers embezzled money, and cops looted drugs from the evidence room—all to feed their addiction. (And don't think it's not an addiction: I've seen guys get their arms and legs busted to "help" them pay debts to their bookies. In the hospital they go. They get splinted and plastered up and they're back on the street, gambling with another bookie, the same day. You're gonna tell me there isn't something cracked in that person's head? Or maybe broken in his heart?) It affects people of all races, ages, and sexes. Don't kid yourself. Nobody is immune.

I'm not proud of my past. I regret and renounce a lot of it. But that doesn't mean you shouldn't get the benefit. If you'd seen what I've seen, you'd want to get it out in the open too.

Understand this: I'm not attacking the gambling industry. I'm not providing moral commentary about whether a person should gamble. You're a grownup. Sort it out on your own. What I am doing is providing perspective that should prevent the gambling from popping a hole in your prosperity.

Machiavelli thought gambling to be such a danger to society in his day that he advised his prince to use it as a weapon against his enemies. "A ruler should encourage gambling among his enemies, and put it down by military force at home." That was before anyone could gamble online or play video poker. Get them gambling among themselves, Machiavelli reasoned, and they would be easier to crush and defeat. He might even recruit bookmakers to work the enemy streets. He didn't stop there. To ensure that his own subjects weren't corrupted by the ancient games of chance, Machiavelli encouraged his prince to use military force, if necessary, to prevent them from gambling. That's some serious smack. (And you wonder where mobsters got the idea for baseball bats and cement shoes?) The mob embraced this philosophy with the intensity of a bone-crushing bear hug (or other bone-crushing things). Gambling has claimed more victims and victories for the mob than any other weapon in its arsenal.

Foul Ball!

In the past twelve years, I have spoken to thousands of people about the possible dangers a gambling issue can pose to all types of businesses. One industry in particular, sports, is known for its gambling appeal. Betting happens not only by outside spectators, but inside the industry itself, which as you might guess is a problem. Does the name Pete Rose mean anything to you? For this reason, owners and directors of those enterprises recruit me, an ex-mobster and onetime threat to their livelihoods, to speak to their most valuable assets (players, coaches, referees, umpires) for the primary purpose of protecting the integrity of their businesses against their most dreaded threat.

In 2007, NBA referee Tim Donaghy was accused of fixing NBA games. David Stern, the normally self-assured and eloquent twenty-three-year commissioner of the NBA, said sheepishly, "I can tell you that this is the most serious . . . and worst situation that I have ever experienced either as a fan of the NBA, a lawyer for the NBA or a commissioner of the NBA. . . . This is . . . the worst that could happen to a professional sports league."

To the commissioner's credit, the NBA has since taken further steps to prevent another betting scandal like this from happening again. But you can be sure that regardless of what actions Stern or the bosses of any other professional or college sports enterprise might take, their businesses will always remain vulnerable. That's because the employees and everyone associated with those businesses also remain vulnerable, as do those who just might be employed by you.

And who were the accused behind the accused in the NBA betting scandal? You guessed it: none other than the boys in the pinstriped suits. Mobsters can smell a person's gambling weakness like a shark can smell blood.

I have since spoken to the disgraced referee. For whatever

the reason I feel bad for him. When it came to his propensity to gamble, he just might have been given an offer he couldn't refuse. And for all of you who believe gambling on sports is a "good bet," get this: the feds allege that Donaghy bet on more than one hundred games over which he officiated from 2003 through the 2007 season when he left the game. Donaghy has since pleaded guilty to betting on games he officiated and providing inside information to others so they would have an edge in betting on NBA games. He was sentenced to fifteen months in federal prison, followed by three years probation, and ordered to pay restitution. You think he might have blown a few extra whistles to protect his bets? Hope none of you had money riding on one of those games.

Bad for Business

Clearly, the governing bodies in all of professional and college sports have educational, investigative, and enforcement policies in place for the sole purpose of protecting the integrity of their respective sports from those who would seek to profit by manipulating the outcome of an event for their advantage. They even go to the extreme of bringing in an ex-mobster to help keep the games honest.

Many of you are probably saying to yourselves, it doesn't take a brain surgeon to understand why sporting enterprises are concerned with gambling. But nobody's betting money on my business. It's unlikely a bookie will take action on which restaurant flips the best burger. Vegas won't give odds on who boasts the prettiest showroom or who sells the most appliances.

And there's no over/under on which gas station posts the best price per gallon or what a movie will gross at the box office, at least none that I am aware of. Let me tell you where the real concerns lie between the problem of gambling and the impact on your business.

A few months ago, I gave a presentation to a group of about seven hundred concerned members of a church congregation in Nashville, Tennessee. It is customary for me to remain on-site to sign books and talk with people after a speaking event. I have had many business owners share stories with me of how their businesses were compromised, in some instances seriously so, due to a gambling problem involving one or more of their employees, or at times even by themselves.

On this particular evening I met a guy who owned a small technology company employing 175 workers. He told me that his business hired an Internet filtering company to do a security scan on all of the company's computers. They observed the business for one month. He was shocked to learn the results of the investigation. Approximately 3,800 hours of company time were spent on gambling sites in one month alone. His accounting department extrapolated the cost to the company of the wasted hours in terms of the lost productivity of his employees over a twelve-month period. They determined that the company had footed the bill for his employees to gamble on company time to the tune of a whopping $1,500,000. In addition, the company had to hire the monitoring company at a considerable expense to install software that would block gambling sites from all of the employees' computers. And this expense does not take into account whatever losses his employees might have suffered as a result of their gambling. The guy openly questioned whether or not those employees might have somehow compromised his business to make up for those losses.

Get you thinking a little bit? How many techie bookies do you have in your office? Right at this minute? You probably never realized you had a casino sitting on your employees' desks. Let me provide you with a few more examples of how gambling can turn even the most reliable employee into a desperate and sometimes frightening one-armed bandit. In every instance that follows, an employee stole or embezzled money from his or her company to feed a gambling obsession.

It Can Happen to You

A local attorney charged with embezzling money from clients for gambling might have stolen far beyond their original estimate of $1.1 million. More clients are coming forward with claims that he cheated them out of money.

DETROIT NEWS

A Comerica Bank manager with nearly 40 years on the job has pleaded guilty to embezzling $1.56 million, all lost at the slots. "I just got obsessed with gambling. Couldn't stay out of the casinos."

GAZETTE NEWS SERVICE

The 69-year-old former president and chief operating officer of Conbraco Industries who lost a fortune after years of struggling to control his gambling addiction, pleaded guilty

to fraudulently obtaining loans that prosecutors say he used
to help pay off more than $30 million in gambling debts.

CHARLOTTE OBSERVER

A 66-year-old grandmother from New York City was sentenced yesterday to 31 months in federal prison and ordered
to pay back the nearly $4.9 million she embezzled from her
former employer to feed her gambling habit in Atlantic City.

PHILLYNEWS.COM

A head cashier for the St. Louis County recorder of deeds
stole about $863,000 from Investors Title Company Inc. by
overcharging and pocketing the difference. Authorities allege
that she took from $200 to $1,200 a day starting in 1995. The
money was spent on gambling debts.

ST. LOUIS POST-DISPATCH

I've got nothing to back up my assumption here, but I'd bet
that none of these gamblers engaged in any type of criminal
conduct prior to acquiring their obsessive gambling habits.
These aren't mobsters in disguise.

You'll find more and more of these stories if you pay attention. None of these people fit the normal criminal profile. The
Comerica Bank manager was on the job nearly forty years. He
had to be doing something right to last that long. Yet forty years
of service went down the drain along with a $1.56 million loss
to his company as a result of his gambling obsession. And sixty-
six-year-old grandmothers don't embezzle money from their
companies to feed their newly acquired drug habits. They don't
become arsonists, bank robbers, or ax murders. But gambling

can be an equal-opportunity destroyer, available to all takers regardless of their age, color, creed, or gender.

It's easy to see how their offenses could have gone undetected so long, even by savvy and responsible business owners. Usually, even when discovered, the news doesn't go beyond the company. Quite often these incidents go unnoticed by anyone but the victims. That doesn't mean it doesn't happen every day. I have seen gamblers destroy what were once healthy, viable companies many more times than I would like to remember. As a business owner or operator, large or small, gambling in all its various forms should be an activity you approach with caution or not at all.

Since I began addressing the gambling issue several years ago, I must admit I was very surprised by the number of women who now engage in some form of gambling. Women didn't seek out bookmakers when I was on the street. I don't recall ever having an issue with a woman gambler. If I had, I would have let her off the hook. I am a bit old-fashioned. I afford women a higher level of respect and courtesy than I would a guy in a similar situation. I don't like to see a woman in a tight spot.

But, no doubt about it, there is an increased number of women gambling today. For some, it's compulsive. The reason for the increase is easily explained: easy access, plus the fact that gambling is now acceptable and no longer carried on in the shadows. Women gamblers don't typically wager with bookmakers. They gamble legally.

This poses an additional problem for the business owner/ operator with respect to his or her female employees. A woman who is a compulsive gambler is much harder to identify than her male counterpart. Women tend to begin gambling at a later, more mature age then men. They are much more discreet about their gambling habits, preferring not to brag about their winnings or make their losses known. They are able to conceal their compulsiveness better and longer than a man; therefore, their gambling problem is exposed at a later time. But for the compulsive gambler, the need to bet becomes the primary thought in her life. She might even turn to crime to obtain money to cover her inevitable losses, and if she is in a position to steal money from the business, she goes for it. By the time the problem is exposed, she has already inflicted substantial damage on the business and on herself. Don't get me wrong: it's true for guys too. They'll nick a dime or a grand as fast as anyone.

In most of the cases just mentioned, the business was the primary victim. Because there are no apparent physical signs of an employee's obsessive gambling habits, the gambling and pilfering of the companies go largely unnoticed for quite some time. By the time the larceny is uncovered, the businesses have taken a major financial hit. It is critical for every business owner and manager to be on the alert and to watch closely even the most honest, loyal, and trustworthy employee.

Keep Your Eye on the Ball

> Know well the condition of your flock, and pay attention to
> your herds, for wealth is not forever; not even a crown lasts
> for all time.
>
> SOLOMON

The proliferation of gambling in society has made it a viable threat to business owners and operators everywhere, especially during times of a slowing economy. Keep gambling on the radar screen of things to watch out for as you operate your business.

Pay close attention to your employees and what's going on in your business!

Gambling is now woven into the fabric of our society. It is a multibillion-dollar (and growing) industry, as much a part of American culture as baseball and apple pie. A few summers ago, I was invited to speak at a seminar attended by officials from the security divisions of all the professional sports leagues. An FBI agent who spoke before me made a statement that warrants repeating. He said, "Baseball is no longer America's national pastime. Gambling is!"

Business owners today operate within this gambling culture. It would be wise to recognize it as a possible threat. A gambling problem in your business, your own or that of an employee, can derail its success with the throw of the dice, the turn of a card, or a threat from some guys having names like Frankie "the Beast," Carmine "the Snake," or Tony "the Ant." Imagine introducing one of them as your partner at the company's annual board meeting. Maybe you already have—and just don't know it yet.

GET THE MESSAGE

1. Don't roll the dice on your business. A gambling issue—whether your own, your partner's, one of your employee's, or even that of a stranger's on the street—can impact your business and your life in a big way. Machiavelli thought gambling to be such a danger to society that he advised his prince to use it as a weapon against his enemies.

2. Online gambling drains a business's resources. How many techie bookies do you have in your office right this minute? Hire an online filtering company to do a security scan on your company's computers today and consider installing software to block gambling sites from all employees' computers.

3. Gambling can be an equal opportunity destroyer, available to all takers regardless of their age, color, creed, or gender.

CHAPTER EIGHT

Learn from Your Failures

As a soldier and capo in the Colombo family, it was a rare day when one of my crew, an associate, or a businessperson failed to propose a deal of some sort. Some of the offers were good, others were bad, and some were just plain ridiculous. As a result, I honed a keen instinct for a cherry opportunity. But good instincts won't save you from every bad deal. And if you haven't made a bad deal, you just haven't made enough deals yet.

Gotti and the Swap Meet

Take the case of the gentleman who was part owner of a "swap meet" in Brooklyn. An accountant by trade, he decided to partner with another in this particular venture. Swap meets were potential cash cows back in the 1980s. An owner was provided several different revenue streams as a landlord, merchant, advertising agent, and money lender. But this accountant's revenue streams had sprung a leak. He learned his partner was stealing from him. Worse, he was using the market to deal drugs. The accountant tried to deal his partner out of the business but failed. So he came to me.

Accountants are good with numbers. Mob guys are good at dealing with thieving drug dealers. Reporting his partner to the police might have resulted in the market being closed down, so he came to me for direction. That's an option available to executives in a city where there is a formidable mob presence.

His proposal: "Get rid of the drug dealer and become my partner in the business." After conducting a brief analysis of both the accountant and the market, I decided to accept. Now the clincher, of course, was how I would convince the drug dealer to walk away from the business. I would—you guessed it!—make him an offer he couldn't refuse. Turns out, my analysis of both the accountant and the business was right on target. But my analysis couldn't account for what came next.

Within a few weeks, none other than the "Dapper Don" himself called me. Apparently, the dealer forgot to mention that he was Gotti's guy when he accepted my offer and scrammed. Get real, right? That's because he *wasn't* Gotti's guy at the time. But in the mobbed-up streets of Brooklyn, it wasn't difficult for a businessman to find a godfather when he needed one.

"The guy's with me, Michael," said the less-than-forthright Dapper Don. "We gotta sit down."

I knew what was coming. Gotti would tell me the dealer was his guy, and through him he would claim ownership in the business. He would assure me that from that point on his guy would be on his best behavior. No more dealing. His hand would stay out of the cookie jar, and everything would be peachy keen. Gotti knew there was money to be earned in the market, and he wasn't about to pass up the opportunity to get a piece.

The sit-down would be a battle of wits. Here's what would happen. I would accuse Gotti of claiming the drug dealer only after I removed him from the market. He would say he knew him since birth. I would counter that even if he did know him, he was a drug dealer; therefore Gotti could have no claim to him. It was common knowledge that drugs were off-limits to made guys. They couldn't use them, deal them, or be in business with anyone dealing them. It was a longstanding policy adopted by all five New York families. Violation was serious.

"What violation?" Gotti would argue that the guy wasn't really a dealer, that he only made a mistake, and that he would see to it himself that from that point on the alleged peddler would be on his best street behavior.

I had known Gotti for quite some time. Most of us mob guys have inflated egos—John's was supersized. Surrendering his claim at the sit-down would have been tantamount to a defeat. I lost. Gotti wouldn't budge.

This was a significant failure for me. My guy couldn't get along with the dealer. (Contrary to Gotti's assertion, he had a pretty lengthy history of drug dealing.) The vendors and merchants didn't like him either. Simply put, this guy was bad for the business. And although I liked Gotti personally and respected him as a made guy, I really had no desire to be in business with him. I could have demanded a sit-down with our bosses for a final decision on the matter. John and I both had juice in the family. A decision could have gone either way, or more likely resulted in a compromise. But that wasn't a battle worth fighting.

My failure to persuade Gotti to walk was frustrating. Partnership wasn't an option. So after conferring with the accountant, I decided to tell Gotti that one of us would have to buy the other out. I made him an offer I knew he *would* refuse and then sold the business to Gotti instead.

Machiavelli would have labeled the outcome a total failure on my part because I failed to exert power and exercise control of the situation. His objective was always to exert power, maintain control, and to be held in high esteem in the eyes of the people. Anything short of meeting those objectives by whatever means necessary would have been considered failure. But it happens. People fail.

Gotti found that out. He bought us out for six figures. The accountant made a profit, I made a good score for my troubles, and Gotti kept the business. It fell apart three months later. I got lucky.

Failure Is Normal

I've not always been so lucky. Over the course of my life, I have failed more times than I have succeeded. Businesses, relationships, sports, finances—you name it, and I have failed in it somewhere along the line. And many of my failures have been highly visible and even humiliating. People notice indictments, jail sentences, closed businesses, and dwindling bank balances.

But here's the good news. Everyone fails. It's normal. It's predictable.

In the age of the Internet, all anyone needs is an idea, a few hundred bucks, and a Web site, and you can call your dot-com a business. It sounds simple enough, but it's not. Too many would-be entrepreneurs find that out after a considerable loss of time and money. There is a reason why the greater percentage of business startups will fail within the first two years of operation.

Think of how many restaurants close their doors—or tech firms, or furniture stores, or any news business. Some of the biggest names in business got started by failing first.

Ray Krok failed in real estate before creating McDonald's. Henry Ford's first two automobile businesses crashed. R. H. Macy failed seven times before his store in New York caught a buzz. Akio Morita and Masaru Ibuka sold only a hundred units of an automatic rice cooker that ended up burning the rice; later, they built a cheap tape recorder for Japanese schools, which laid the groundwork for the Sony Corporation. Bill Hewlett and David Packard's early failed products included a lettuce-picking machine and an electric weight-loss apparatus. Walt Disney of all people was fired by the editor of a newspaper because he had "no good ideas."

The list of successful business "failures" is a long one. But that's not the point. Here's what is: The one sure characteristic all of these folks had in common was their willingness to pick themselves off the floor, dust themselves off, and try again. And sometimes again and again and again.

Going to School

It's not how many times a person fails that necessarily matters. It's not called the School of Hard Knocks for nothing—it's all about what you learn. It's what a person learns from failure and how he reacts to it that leads to either ultimate success or ultimate failure. What information can you take away that will benefit you the next time around? What can you learn so you will never repeat the same mistake twice? How will you allow it to affect you internally so you don't give up, but keep on moving forward?

Just think about some of the benefits of failure:

- Failing can show you defects in your plan.
- Failing can reveal defects in the execution or timing of a plan.
- Failing can identify weaknesses in a team that need to be addressed.
- Failing can highlight otherwise undetected variables at play.

I got a good education from the many times I failed, and I'm relatively certain I'm not done yet—failing or learning. Once you assess the situation, you can remedy the gaps in your plan and your execution and improve your performance for the next time out.

When I was released from prison in 1995, I was flat broke. I had spent millions as a result of my past legal issues and the cost of supporting my family through my ten years of imprisonment and parole. I wasted no time in pursuing new business ventures as a means to get back on my feet. No problem, right? After all, according to *Life* magazine, I was the "mob's young genius." Creating a new business empire should be a snap for a man with that kind of moniker. Everything I touched should turn to gold! As it turns out, almost everything I touched involving business turned to ashes. All except the career I was unconsciously building as a speaker, consultant, and author. I found out that being an ex–New York mob guy with a price on his head and on parole was not conducive to establishing a successful business in the

Golden State. In the years following my release from prison, I carried far too much baggage from my past to have a chance at succeeding in any meaningful business venture. Although I had quit the life years earlier, making the transition from a high-profile mobster to a normal, law-abiding businessman would not happen overnight. It took me almost seven years to realize what my new direction in life would be. Two business failures in those years caused me to reassess my plan and to focus on the business that I appeared to be succeeding in. My new plan would be to proceed in that direction with "tunnel vision," refusing to be distracted or sidetracked by any other business opportunity or proposal. My new plan worked. And although there were consequences, both emotional and financial, my business failures once again led to the success I am having in my career today.

This isn't to say that you can improve in every instance after a failure. Sometimes you're just unlucky. Gotti had no idea that the swap meet would fail, any more than I knew the thieving drug dealer would try to push his nose back into my business. Don't forget what Montaigne said about failure and luck (I know he's French, but give him a break):

> I have fallen into some serious and important mistakes in my life, not for lack of good counsel but for lack of good luck. There are secret parts in the matters we handle which cannot be guessed, especially in human nature. . . . If my prudence has been unable to see into them and predict them, I bear it no ill will; its responsibility is restricted within its limitations. It is the outcome that beats me; and if it favors the course I have refused, there is no help for it; I do not blame myself; I accuse my luck, not my work.

If it's just a question of luck, then don't beat yourself down. If your idea was good, then stay on it. But don't fool yourself either. Maybe the lesson is something you don't want to hear. "If at first you don't succeed, quit. Don't be a damn fool about it." W. C. Fields when he said that wasn't endorsing chickening out. He was saying don't waste time and energy doing something you're bad at.

Not Everyone Can Be a Mobster

I'm convinced that if La Cosa Nostra were an equal opportunity employer, there wouldn't be enough criminal activity to perpetrate to support all its members. You would not believe how many men would kill (no pun intended) to get their buttons and join the ranks. Fortunately, membership in the life is considered by its members to be a privilege. There is a screening process for all perspective members. In order to be considered for induction, a prospect must be deemed to have the qualities it takes to succeed in the life. And that's a good thing for the law-abiding citizen. There are a lot fewer criminals on the streets to be concerned about. For the wannabe mobster who just might not make the grade, it's even a better thing. Recruiting a guy who isn't qualified won't get him fired. It will get him whacked. The mob doesn't believe in severance packages.

There is a big lie in our society today, a lie we feed our young people in an effort to evangelize for the latest religion of our day—"the religion of self-esteem." I visit middle and high schools to speak to the students. I can't tell you how many times I've seen banners stretched across an auditorium that say something like:

"You can be whatever you want to be in life." *Bull*. Simply not true. If I could have been whatever I wanted to be in life, I would have been playing centerfield for the Yankees. Mickey Mantle was my idol. But there was a big problem: I was good, sure, but not *that* good. Filling our young people with false hopes and unrealistic goals will end up being far more damaging to their self-esteem. We should encourage kids to explore their individual talents and develop those gifts into their future vocation.

> It is a trap for a man to dedicate something rashly and only later to consider his vows.
>
> SOLOMON

It's not just schools. I coached Little League baseball and had to contend with demanding parents who insisted that their child play a certain position that he was in no way capable of playing. Why? Because his self-esteem would be damaged if he couldn't. Of course, they never considered the blow to his self-esteem when he made an error, blew the game, and his teammates rebuked him for it. Not every player is qualified to play every position on the field.

What's true in school and on the field is doubly true in business. Not everyone is qualified to run a business. Some of us are better employees and workers than we are owners or operators. The worker who can effectively service a car's tires and brakes can't always effectively service the responsibilities of the business that brought the car into the shop. I have seen many skilled workers become bad business operators. It takes management skills, among other things, to steer a business successfully. Not everyone has them, nor can everyone acquire them. And that's not necessarily a bad thing. It's always better to stick with what you do best and let others do the rest.

Failure is a tough teacher, but it can teach us our strengths and weaknesses in ways no other teacher can.

It was through my failures that I discovered what I was good at and what I was not so good at. I learned how to do what I do best and delegate the rest whenever possible. Identifying and accepting both my strengths and weaknesses was an important factor to the successes of my business operations. For example, I'm not a detail-oriented guy. I don't like getting involved in the day-to-day minutiae that is an integral part of any organization or business venture. I'm just not good at it and, frankly, don't really like handling those kinds of responsibilities. However, I know what needs to be done, and I am very capable delegating those tasks to others who are better and more qualified to deal with them, and holding them accountable in their performance. In doing so, I give myself a far better chance of succeeding in that particular situation than if I were to try to manage those things myself.

Don't Take It on the Lam!

Q. What do you call it when the FBI reads sixty-one Gambino crime family members and their associates their Miranda rights?
A. An offer they can't refuse.

It was ugly. One of the biggest racketeering indictments ever thrown at a mob family. And this paper tiger had teeth. The early morning raid in February 2008 was well planned.

The feds caught all but one of the unsuspecting mobsters in their pajamas.

Gambino caporegime Nicholas "Little Nicky" Corozzo got away. He was tipped off about the raid, managed to shed his pajamas, and took it on the lam before the feds could bring him his silver bracelet. After a few months on the lam, Little Nicky decided to surrender to the authorities. A featured piece on *America's Most Wanted*, along with the willingness of the feds to cut him a deal, apparently caused him to reassess his situation and trade his running shoes in for an orange jumpsuit.

What does all of this have to do with the price of a meatball hero? *Nothing!* But it has everything to do with facing the music when your business is hurting. Fact is, your business will go through tough times. Finances will be short, and creditors and suppliers will be at your doorstep, hands out, palms up, itching to collect. Do yourself a favor: Answer the door. Forget about the circumstances. Forget about whether you can pay. Don't avoid your creditors. It may hurt (more than just your pocketbook), and it may be unpleasant, but talk to the boys to whom you owe money. It's a must.

Communication builds confidence. More often than not, your creditors will be willing to create payment arrangements for you. They want you to stay afloat. They lose if you close up shop. Being available and cooperative shows creditors that you are not running away from the debt. You're in it with them, you take responsibility, and you'll do whatever necessary to keep your business alive in tough times. An aging gangster facing a thousand years in prison might get some value out of going on the lam, but that's a no-go for business owners trying to achieve and maintain success.

There's an ancient story about a Greek general who landed his troops on an enemy shore and then burned his own ships. He wanted to make it very clear to his troops that retreat and failure were not options. Facing your creditors will demonstrate your commitment to creating success, and, more often than not, in doing so you will make them your ally.

An honest businessperson should not feel shamed if he or she experiences financial problems in a business. Next to sickness and death, financial issues are probably the most stressful problems to deal with in life. Oftentimes pride and embarrassment stand in the businessperson's way of facing the financial crisis head-on. Running away will not make the crisis go away. Deal with it face-to-face. Don't be a dummy: Use every legal protection available if necessary. But don't be a bigger dummy: Deal with it. Don't take it on the lam!

If you falter in times of trouble, how small is your strength.

SOLOMON

Take It to Heart

King Solomon was greater in riches than all other kings of the earth in his day. He received close to fifty thousand pounds of gold *a year* from his subjects, not to mention the gold he amassed from trade. He had so much of it, in fact, that silver wasn't even valuable during his lifetime. Even his plates and cups were made of pure gold. Solomon possessed enough wealth to make any modern-day ruler wonder, *What if I lose all of this? What if something happens to all my wealth? What if I am a* financial failure? And yet, any reader of the writings of Solomon can easily discern that, at least in his early years, the wise king was much more concerned with moral and spiritual failure—that of the heart and soul—than with material failure. This is, perhaps, a helpful perspective to consider when our failure to turn a profit begins to bog us down. No matter what the pressure, we must keep our internal lives in check and in good health. That way, when tangible failures do come, we have a strong foundation of core values on which to stand. From there, not only can we recover; we can move ahead.

Thankfully the business world—brutal as it may be—is not as brutal about failure as is the underworld. When it comes to business, the mob life leaves very little room for error and even less room for excuses. Fail once at something small and you are sure to draw a severe tongue lashing from your superior. Fail a few times at something small and you will be "placed on the shelf," a designated non-earner, relegated to handling the family's less-desirable "business." Fail at something major and you might very well be invited into a room with no exit. The mob life taught me how to dispense with excuses, recover quickly from failure, and get it right the next time—or else. Perhaps this was a far less conventional way to learn that failure should only provide a stronger motivation to succeed. It was, nonetheless, effective.

Failure isn't falling down; it's staying down. Like Old Blue Eyes sang in "That's Life":

Each time I find myself laying flat on my face
I just pick myself up and get back in the race.

GET THE MESSAGE

1. When you fail, pick yourself up off the floor, dust yourself off, and try again.

2. Failure can: show you the defects in your plan, reveal the defects in the execution or timing of a plan, identify weaknesses in a team that need to be addressed, or highlight otherwise undetected variables at play.

3. You can't always just improve the plan after a failure. Sometimes you're just unlucky! If it's a question of luck, then don't beat yourself down. If you're bad at something, don't waste your time and energy fooling yourself. If your idea was good, then stay on it.

4. Failure is a tough teacher, but it can teach you your strengths and weaknesses in a way that no other teacher can.

5. Don't avoid your creditors. Your business will go through tough times, but running away is not the answer. Deal with the crisis head-on. It may be unpleasant; it may hurt your pride; it may be embarrassing; but don't be a dummy. Talk to the boys to whom you owe money. It's a must.

CHAPTER NINE

Play It Straight and Legal

Nobody wants to fail. Some would rather cheat than lose. I get the feeling that many corporate executives and business owners have been reading their Machiavelli. They think almost anything goes as long as you don't get caught.

> . . . and in the actions of all men, and especially of princes, which it is not prudent to challenge, one judges by the result.
>
> MACHIAVELLI

Judges by the result. Another translation gets to the heart of that phrase: "the end justifies the means." This quote most accurately sums up Machiavelli's entire philosophy. Almost any action—legal or criminal, moral or immoral—is kosher so long as it serves to further one's interest in the end. It's a questionable philosophy to live by, at best, and a dangerous framework within which to conduct a business.

If you play the game by these rules, you'll lose in the end. Nothing derails success like a grand jury investigation. But lost consumer trust hurts too. This is what comes from allowing ends to justify means. And, unlike businesses that fail after honest efforts, enterprises that crash and burn due to fraudulent activity usually reap nasty and sometimes brutal consequences.

I assume that most of you reading this book have not been inducted into an organized criminal organization. That being the case, I will also assume that you have no intention to deliberately engage in any fraudulent activity in your business, which normally involves some form of theft or deceitful representation, for the purpose of obtaining money of your product or service.

Business fraud is considered a "white-collar" crime. Although I was charged with a number of white-collar crimes within the body of my racketeering indictments, they are usually perpetrated by professionals, businesspeople, and public officials. Most white-collar offenders are ordinary people, not mob soldiers, who for a multitude of reasons make rash or uncharacteristically poor decisions. Sometimes they see their way out of financial difficulty through illegal and fraudulent means. Other times they just see an opportunity to make money by perpetrating a scheme, as I did with my gas cartel. In either case it's wrong. Although short-term benefits of engaging in such activity might seem appealing, they will be far outweighed by the consequences both you and your business will suffer once the illicit activity is exposed.

People who engage in fraudulent business activities do so believing they will never get caught. The executives at Enron, WorldCom, Adelphia, and Global Crossing (to name a few that made national headlines), all perpetrated their frauds thinking that they could do so under some imaginary veil of protection. Make no mistake: Big Brother is watching, and he has plenty of help. Your once trusted employee, your cell phone, the Internet, the mail carrier, your major competitor, or an unhappy customer—all are potentially Big Brother's allies when you have committed a crime. Trust me on this one!

Government's New Tools

I remember flying back to New York from Miami in 1986 while I was in federal custody. I had pleaded guilty to racketeering charges in a Florida courthouse as part of my overall agreement with the feds to resolve charges around the gas-tax scam. I was accompanied by at least ten G-men from the various federal law-enforcement agencies that were part of the investigation that led to my federal indictment in Brooklyn. The agents were in good spirits, realizing the long investigation that finally led to my accepting a plea was coming to an end. At least it was for them. I still had to do the time.

We were sitting in the back of the plane, trading small talk, when an FBI agent asked me a question. Now that the case was resolved, he wanted to know if they had the facts straight in the investigation. Remember, I didn't fight the indictment. Once the horse was out of the gate, everyone jumped in. Agents started peppering me with questions about this or that incident that occurred during the investigation—whether their assumptions were correct.

I toyed with them a bit. "You boys were way off base," I told them. A lot of times they were. I told them about all the times I'd beaten them in the past and how I would have beaten them again if the case had gone to trial. But I was letting Uncle Sam win one for a change. Big of me, right? I was jerking their chains a bit, having a little fun at the agents' expense. I will never forget what one agent told me that day.

"Not this time," he said. "You're now a get-out-of-jail-card for every guy on the street looking to make a deal. Witnesses were lining up to testify against you this time around." He wasn't jerking my chain. He was telling the truth.

That's the way things have gone in the mob since the mid-1980s. Made guys turn informant left and right. More so today than at any other time in the history of organized crime. The popular reason given for this trend is that the younger mobsters are not as disciplined and can't take the heat the way the old-timers could. Not true. Here's the real reason: The government has more weapons to fight organized crime today than ever before. The laws are tougher, and there are more of them on the books. The prison sentences are much more severe and there is no longer a chance to make parole. Al Capone was sentenced to fifteen years in prison for tax violations in the early 1930s. He made parole after serving seven years. Today he would probably be sentenced to fifty years in prison and would be required to do 85 percent of his time in the joint. Don't believe the myths. This isn't the 1920s, and I doubt mobsters of earlier generations could stand up any better in that situation than the mobsters of today.

Some of you might be thinking that you need not worry about all of this since your business doesn't resemble a mob family. You're no mobster, right? Not so fast. Criminal pedigree doesn't matter like it used to.

As a result of the wave of massive corporate fraud that began in the 1990s, the government has declared war on corporate executives who scoff at the law. Congress has empowered the Justice Department with a slew of new laws, and it has made significant progress in dealing with the problem over the years. Several high-profile arrests and indictments of corporate executives from major companies, both public and private, have resulted in convictions of the executives and massive fines and penalties to the businesses involved in the frauds. And for those of you who operate a small business and believe you can fly under the government's radar, I caution you to beware. Unless you conduct your business in a vacuum or in total isolation, someone is always watching. You might get away with it once or twice. You *might*! But I assure you, if you make a habit of it, you will be exposed. And once you are, you're toast!

Through the White House's Corporate Fraud Task Force, the DOJ, SEC, CFTC, FCC, and IRS are working together more closely than ever to drop the hammer on offenders. Corporate fraud on almost any level is getting moblike treatment from the Justice Department. The sentences being handed down by the courts on those executives convicted of fraud are moblike for sure. Jeff Skilling of Enron got twenty-five years in prison; Bernie Ebbers of WorldCom got twenty-five years; and Tyco's Dennis Kozlowski, of the six-thousand-dollar shower-curtain fame, got eight to twenty-five years.

Because of the recent real estate bust, the FBI is focusing its efforts on the mortgage industry. Since mortgage fraud is a federal offense, the FBI is investigating all possible instances. Fraud for profit is usually perpetrated by an industry insider and sometimes referred to as "Industry Insider Fraud." The motive is to revolve equity, falsely inflate the value of the property, or issue loans based on fictitious properties. Current investigations and mortgage fraud reporting shows that 80 percent of all reported fraud losses involve collaboration or collusion by industry insiders, business owners, and operators.

I know from experience there are no shortages of business-people who are ready, willing, and able to circumvent the law by defrauding their own company, a competing company, or individuals for personal gain when the opportunity arises. As of the time of this writing, all indications are that the aftermath of the real-estate debacle is going to string on for quite a while, creating further opportunity for a business to profit by engaging in fraudulent practices.

I told you earlier that I was involved in the auto business. I had an arrangement with the CEO of a Small Business Investment Company (SBIC). Call him Mr. X. His business was licensed by the federal Small Business Administration (SBA) to lend money to small businesses. When Mr. X agreed to provide a $250,000 credit line to my Mazda dealership, without so much as a credit check, he did so with one condition. Aside from the interest payment due on the loan, I would pay him a "consulting fee" of between $75 and $150 on every vehicle sold. There was no consulting service provided. The fee was bogus. It was a way for Mr. X to earn more money than he was allowed to under SBA guidelines at the time. I signed a bogus consulting agreement and paid him that fee for years. The dealership was selling as many as fifty cars per month. The money he was paid was substantial.

Mr. X and his company eventually came under investigation by either law enforcement or the SBA. I can't recall which. I was questioned about the consulting fee. They wanted to know if it was legitimate and if Mr. X was really providing the service. They were clearly interested in pursuing the matter. They told me that if the fee was bogus, Mr. X would have to repay me all the money I paid him over the years. Of course I told them he was providing the service, but had I told them it was bogus, there is no doubt in my mind he would have been in the dog's jaws, if you know what I mean.

Another corporate executive—call him Mr. Y—got me out from under the "consulting fees" I was paying Mr. X. Mr. Y, who had relatives associated with the mob, came through for me with a $600,000 line of credit for my dealership. Instead of having to pay Mr. X his consulting fee, I negotiated to pay Mr. Y a third of that. But with Mr. Y we didn't fool around with "consulting." His payments went straight under the table, a table his employer was unaware of. He earned plenty of money at that table. He needed every penny for his lawyers. Mr. Y was indicted along with me and several others in Brooklyn federal court for racketeering and fraud. He ended up being convicted and sentenced to two years in the federal pen.

These are only two of several instances where seemingly legitimate businesspeople that I personally did business with were willing to engage in fraudulent activity for personal gain. I had similar experiences with other finance people, bankers, casino executives, travel agents, stockbrokers, union officials, insurance company executives, and government employees. Prosecutors would later claim that my greatest talent was in finding legitimate businessmen who liked to play on the edge. They only got it half right. I did know how to work them once they came to me. However, contrary to popular perception, mobsters do not have to search these people out. In each and every case, these businesspeople approached me with a scheme to defraud their company. Eventually, they all paid a price.

Temptations to engage in shady practices will always present themselves to the business owner/operator. Some of you might consider engaging in such conduct, possibly out of greed or a genuine desire to keep a sinking business afloat. In either case, it is wrong, and you will end up paying for it in the end. "Food gained by fraud tastes sweet to a man," said Solomon, "but he ends up with a mouth full of gravel." When it comes to your business, play by the rules and the laws that are in place to enforce them or you may learn that prison food is not much tastier than gravel.

Render to Caesar the Things
That Are Caesar's . . . Like Taxes!

On a particular day in 1988, I was sitting in the prison cell I had called home for the last three years, waiting for the highlight of my day—mail call. Not a day went by without receiving a letter from my lovely wife. The kids were great too. Their artistic talents were prominently displayed on the walls of my cell. This time, I also received a letter from the Internal Revenue Service. I threw it on the bottom of my pile and decided to open it after returning from dinner. I would rather deal with the IRS on a full stomach. Just before hitting the sack, I opened the letter. After reading it I laughed out loud. They claimed I owed more than fifty million dollars in back taxes from my illegal earnings in the gas business. How did they arrive at that figure?

Apparently, every time a witness in a gasoline–tax-related

case claimed he handed me money, I was taxed for it. There were no records, no documents, no bank accounts, no tax returns. The uncorroborated testimony of government witnesses was all it took to charge me with the debt. But that's not what made me laugh. I definitely didn't find that part of the letter very funny. What made me laugh were the methods of payment offered at the bottom of the page. The coupon suggested the following: Visa, MasterCard, or American Express. Had I had access to my credit card, I would have filled in the number and sent it in.

I received that letter some twenty years ago, along with several dozen more in the years that followed. I have been through just about every collection procedure the IRS has in its arsenal. It has taken me twenty years to come to an agreement with them. Their memory is longer than a herd of elephants. I had better luck surviving a mob death sentence than I did avoiding the collection efforts of the IRS.

I am not whining here. My tax issues were self-imposed. I chose to live according to the Machiavellian philosophy. The IRS was well within its rights to pursue collection efforts against me. And pursue it did. Relentlessly. I will tell you this, however: when I decided to stop avoiding their collection efforts and meet them head-on, I found the agents I worked with to be very responsive. When they realized I was no longer trying to avoid collection, I noticed a distinct change in their attitudes. While I can't promise that everyone who owes back taxes will experience the kinder and gentler transition that I did, I can say that avoiding the IRS will only serve to make its collection efforts stronger. They have a number of weapons that they will not hesitate to use against you. The fewer your business experiences, the better.

If you want to achieve and maintain success in your business, *pay your taxes*! I'm not telling you to pay more than you owe, but do pay every cent the law requires. Wealthy businesspeople do not haggle over nickels and dimes. They invest their dollars to make millions! If you can legally avoid taxes, go for it! Use the law to your advantage when you can. But cooking the books to hide income or save a few bucks with the IRS will eventually get you and your business cooked.

Cook the Pasta, Not the Books

Mob guys are great with numbers, especially when the numbers concern money that is due them. Most mob guys can account for every penny owed to them from a hundred different sources and never have to write down a single number. It's all in their heads. They don't get Alzheimer's disease; they have great memories. If you want to improve your memory, do it the mob way—lend someone money.

For mobsters, business ledgers and records end up as evidence in a courtroom, so why bother? They don't have to worry about cooking the books in their business. Mob guys can stick to making their pasta al dente. But unless your business is a loan-sharking or bookmaking operation, you need to take a hands-on approach to accounting and keep good records. You gotta know the numbers!

Aside from the obvious benefit of getting a better feel for the progress, or lack thereof, of your business, keeping good records will allow you to detect and put a stop to any dubious activities that might be taking place *before* they spiral out of control—like gambling; don't forget the lessons of chapter 7. Donald Trump likes to say, "If you don't know every aspect of what you are doing, down to the paper clips, you're setting yourself up for some unwelcome surprises." It's some sound advice from a man whose money can buy a few billion paper clips. Take it from The Donald. When it comes to accounting for every dollar that goes in and out of your company's coffers, you better be sure you sweat the small stuff!

Keep one set of books, and keep them straight. Confine your cooking to the food in your pots and not the numbers in your QuickBooks program. You might put on a few pounds, but your business won't go broke, and you won't get fitted for an orange jumpsuit.

> Dishonest scales are detestable to the LORD, but an accurate weight is His delight.
>
> SOLOMON

In other words, God hates cheaters; He loves it when people deal square.

There is no question that tougher laws and more aggressive enforcement have had an impact on corporate accounting measures. The 2002 Sarbanes-Oxley Act requires companies to set up comprehensive internal controls, and it established a new federal board to oversee the auditors of these companies. As a result of the high-profile convictions of corporate executives from major companies, top executives must now personally sign off on company financial statements so they can no longer pass the buck to their subordinates for cooking the books. Bernard Ebbers was convicted of an $11 billion accounting scandal that capsized WorldCom. Jeff Skilling was convicted of, among other things, cooking the books at Enron. Adelphia Communications founder John Rigas and his son were convicted of crimes that included fraudulent accounting procedures. The list goes on and on. Businesspeople, beware. Big Brother is watching. Restrict your cooking to the kitchen and the backyard barbecue.

Integrity Always Matters

Being Machiavellian need not imply manipulation, cruelty, or hostility for its own sake. But the Machiavellian is sure willing, if need be. In *The Prince*, Machiavelli did not discount the use of "villainy" to gain an advantage. He declared that he would not discuss the "merits" of this method.

While Machiavelli explicitly omitted any praise of villainy, he refused to condemn it. Instead, he simply noted that some men will find themselves "obliged" to use such tactics—a tremendously practical and deeply amoral vision of politics! When you apply this concept to business, you have justifiable larcenous and fraudulent business practices, if that's what it takes to achieve and maintain success at the bargaining table; the boardroom; and for mobsters, the sit-down. It's all about winning or losing and not about how you play the game, yet one must always give the appearance of acting with integrity and respect.

Machiavelli claimed that a prince should always seem to have virtues, even if he doesn't actually have them. Moreover, he asserted that seeming to have virtues is actually better than really having them, since a prince is therefore not tied by the bonds of morality. If he does not feel any constraint of "virtue," a prince is better able to do what he needs to do in any given situation. He must, Machiavelli wrote, have a mind "disposed to turn itself about as the winds," able to do good when he can, but also do evil when he must. Still, even though on the inside he is able to scheme, he should appear to be "merciful, faithful, humane, upright, and religious" on the outside.

I came from a life where integrity and honesty in business was the rule only when convenient. I came away from my first sit-down with the impression that it was okay to be dishonest if it would benefit my position. Integrity worked for me on that day, but it might not work for me in the future, and that was okay, I thought. Having integrity was more of a "tactical maneuver" than a philosophy. It was all about winning.

For a mob guy, it was the appearance of integrity that mattered in his business dealings, not integrity itself. When dealing with other mobsters, one always had to appear that he was acting honestly, even when dishonesty was necessary to prevail in an argument or business matter. Remember Mario and the chicken magnates?

Operating without integrity is just bad business, and it should never be confused with engaging in smart business. The two are separate, although the line between them is often blurred. We each have a conscience, and I believe we all know when we cross the line from smart to bad business.

The integrity of the upright guides them, but the unfaithful are destroyed by their duplicity.

SOLOMON

I believe it is safe to assume that many of the companies struggling in today's economy are managed by men and women of integrity. It's also safe to assume that a few are not. The struggles aren't the real issue. Everyone struggles. Nothing guarantees success. But having integrity will make you friends. Along with hard work, experience, the right support staff, and a little luck, it'll *help* you achieve success in business. Without it, your success will be fleeting.

Beating the Greed Monster

Greed. Solomon wrote, "One man gives freely, yet gains even more; another withholds unduly, but comes to poverty." One major principle to keep in mind to help you live your life and run your business with integrity is: keep greed away. Problems are sure to creep up if you refuse to be satisfied with what is probably a good thing already. This is a lesson I learned from Norby Walters, who I talked about in chapter 6.

Greed is a dirty little word in business that packs a powerful punch and will get you every time. You remember Gordon Gekko's speech from *Wall Street*:

> The point is, ladies and gentlemen, that *greed*—for lack of a better word—is good. *Greed* is right. *Greed* works. *Greed* clarifies, cuts through, and captures the essence of the evolutionary spirit. *Greed*, in all of its forms—greed for life, for money, for love, knowledge—has marked the upward surge of mankind.

Terrific movie. Great speech. Also a fantastic lie. Greed almost cost Norby his life. In the end, it still got the better of him. Within a few years of the Stage Deli sit-down, greed finally caught up with him. He ultimately faced a federal indictment, a pile of legal fees, a jury trial, and the eventual loss of his lucrative business. Norby narrowly managed to avoid wearing an orange prison jumpsuit. Last I heard, he was dealing aces to the stars in a weekly poker game in Beverly Hills. I guess some cats really do have nine lives.

Greed is what catapulted Ivan Boesky, the real-life arbitrageur of the Gekko character in *Wall Street*, to a real-life prison. The same can be said for the boys at Enron, Martha Stewart, and countless other big-name CEOs who chose to travel down the primrose path of greed since the turn of this century. Rest assured there will be others to follow.

Despite what Gekko says, greed doesn't clarify. It makes you myopic. Here's proof.

In another book attributed to Solomon, called Ecclesiastes, the king commended investing. "Cast your bread upon the waters," he said, "for after many days you will find it again." In other words, invest and you'll get a return. But listen to what he wrote next: "Give portions to seven, yes, to eight, for you do not know what disaster may come upon the land."

Now, think of all the companies that tied up too much of their capital in mortgage-backed securities or leveraged themselves to the gills with credit default swaps. They didn't follow Solomon's advice. They saw a deal and jumped. Good for them. The problem was that they got greedy. And their greed made it hard for them to objectively weigh the risks. See? They got myopic. All they could see was the payoff. They gave their "portion" to just one or two, and when disaster came upon their land, they were sunk.

Greed is Machiavellian. In *The Prince*, Machiavelli wrote about trickery and greed and how the use of both is justified if it accomplishes one's goals. Greed is as much a part of the mob culture as a .38 caliber pistol. When my gasoline cartel was making me rich well beyond my expectations and I knew the feds were closing in on me, I couldn't give it up. How do you turn off pumps that were spilling out millions of dollars a week? Had I closed it down and got out early, I might have saved myself a stretch in prison and millions of bucks in fines and legal fees. But greed kept me locked in the game. I have been around it all my life. I have seen it swallow up people's lives and those around them.

In business, your desire to succeed and excel should never be overtaken by a greedy motivation to do the same. Greed will do you in. That's a fact. But desire will help you win. A healthy, competitive desire to succeed in business is not only good; it's necessary. But greed has no place in the boardroom or the stockroom. We all have something that motivates us. But if greed is what motivates you, get ready for the hard fall, my friend. A business built on greed is one that is built on sinking sand.

Do the Right Thing

"Do the right thing" is a phrase that is as much a staple of mob lingo as is "fuggedaboutit." If I heard it once, I heard it a thousand times. As a matter of fact, I used the expression about that much. Doing the right thing is important in the mob's business. Of course, the "right thing" in mob business is quite often the wrong thing, and not something you want to practice in your own legitimate business. A mob guy delivering the line would normally follow it with an "or else." For example, a mob lender would tell a borrower late on his interest payment, "Do the right thing, *or else* . . . I'll break your legs." Or when negotiating a contract with a real estate developer: "Do the right thing, *or else* . . . I'll firebomb your building." Just some subtle reminders of how important it is for businessmen to "do the right thing" when dealing with mob guys. For our purposes here we'll define doing the right thing as acting with integrity in all areas of life and business.

In the research study "Does Business Ethics Pay?" conducted by the Institute of Business Ethics (IBE), it was found that companies displaying a "clear commitment to ethical conduct" consistently outperform companies that do not display ethical conduct. The director of IBE, Philippa Foster Back, said, "Not only is ethical behaviour in business life the right thing to do in principle, we have shown that it pays off in financial returns." These findings deserve to be considered a critical baseline for companies to use in the way they conduct themselves.

> He who pursues righteousness and love finds life, prosperity and honor.
>
> SOLOMON

Solomon recognized the value of being trustworthy. He considered it the pathway to prosperity. It should be no surprise that companies that show a clear commitment to ethical conduct outshine, in many ways, those that employ unsavory and shady practices.

The bottom line is that people want to do business with a company they can trust. It's easy to recognize a company that operates with trust as its core. A small business that instills a deep-seated theme of ethics within its strategies and policies will be noticed, appreciated, and valued by its customers. Its overall influence will lead to a profitable, successful company. Those companies that engage in questionable or outright unethical practices will ultimately be exposed and suffer the consequences.

Many of my former mob associates are either dead, in prison, or on their way. Tom Dibella was indicted on federal racketeering charges in the southern district of New York. He died before doing any time. Andrew Russo has been in and out of prison for the better part of the last twenty years. Peter Castellano is no longer strong-arming businesses to buy his putrefied birds. He's believed dead. In December 1986, Big Paul was gunned down in front of Sparks Steak House in Manhattan, on orders from Dapper Don John Gotti, who has since died of cancer while serving a life sentence in federal prison. And you know what happened to me.

> Such are the paths of all who pursue gain dishonestly; it takes the lives of those who profit from it.
>
> SOLOMON

Solomon was saying that if you use deceit as the means to gain, you will lose your life. Take it literally or figuratively: he was right. Men of integrity don't commit to a criminal lifestyle that is rife with deceit and dishonesty, my former self included.

Businessmen and -women of integrity don't cheat their customers or steal from their business partners. There is a price to pay for those of us who choose to navigate the waters of life without integrity, and everyone who chooses that path will have to pay up at some point in time. Guaranteed! The consequences may not be as severe as those suffered by mobsters, but they might be just as devastating in terms of the impact on a person's business and life.

Integrity is not something you pull out of a drawer when it serves your purposes and stuff back in when it doesn't. That's the way of the street. At times, various circumstances that arise in business may cause one to employ that misguided method of the street. Apparently it has been the way for the multitude of corporate executives who, in recent years, have found themselves on the wrong side of the law and who are now on the inside of a prison cell—their lives left in ruins. But it doesn't have to be that way for you

GET THE MESSAGE

1. Don't be like the corporate executives and business owners who think almost anything goes as long as you don't get caught. If you play the game by Machiavelli's rules you'll lose in the end.

2. People who engage in fraudulent business activities do so believing they operate under some imaginary veil of protection. Unless you conduct your business in a vacuum or in total isolation, someone is always watching. You might get away with it once or twice, but I assure you, if you make a habit of it, you will be exposed. Big Brother is watching and you will get caught.

3. Keep good records. Keep one set of books, and keep them straight.

4. Operate with integrity.

5. Everyone struggles. Nothing guarantees success, but having integrity will make you friends. Along with hard work, experience, the right support staff, and a little luck, it'll help you achieve success in business. Without it, you're success will be fleeting.

6. Don't be greedy in your business endeavors. Your desire to succeed and excel should never be overtaken by a greedy motivation to do the same. Greed will do you in, but desire will help you win. A healthy, competitive desire to succeed in business is not only good, it's necessary. If greed is what motivates you, get ready for a hard fall.

7. Can you be trusted? People want to do business with a company they can trust. Companies that engage in questionable or outright unethical practices will ultimately be exposed and suffer the consequences.

CHAPTER TEN

Pick Your Philosopher:
Machiavelli or Solomon?

Having been introduced to Machiavelli and Solomon, now is the time to sit back and think about how you conduct your business (or, if you are just starting out, how you would like to). Do you follow Machiavelli's lead? Or Solomon's?

Don't get ahead of yourself: If you're "with" Machiavelli, that doesn't automatically make you a candidate for a seat at the La Cosa Nostra family table. There are more than a few additional requirements to gain entry into the life. But, hey, if your father is Italian, being a Machiavellian is a good start. That said, operating under the Machiavellian philosophy doesn't make you a bad person by itself. But I can tell you this: if you follow his line of thinking, it does make you susceptible to your own failings and moral corruptions. And it doesn't always take many. Follow Machiavelli, and you may find yourself easily able to justify stepping outside the lines of what is morally and legally acceptable in our society to make your business prosper. Watch out.

Then again, maybe your business follows the Solomon path and you manage your affairs with integrity, steering your course by a reliable moral and legal compass. This isn't to say that your business is managed perfectly. It also doesn't guarantee you success. I've known some upstanding bumblers and failures in my time. But it does show that you are a person with core values and high standards with which you operate. If that's important to you—and I hope it is—then you are on the right path.

Some are wondering if you can have it both ways. A little bit of Machiavelli in one situation, a little Solomon in another. I'm afraid not. Don't get me wrong: these guys are not polar opposites. There are areas of life and business where there's common ground. Even Republicans and Democrats agree on some issues. The difference is that Machiavelli says that "the end justifies the means," and he permits you to do *whatever* it takes to make your business great (even following some of the wisdom of Solomon and faking a moral code). Solomon, however, does not allow you to compromise either your values or your integrity—on which he places a high premium—to be successful. If you are trying to have it both ways, you're just fooling yourself. You're being Machiavellian.

Final Exam Time

Here's a question: Under whose umbrella would you stand in your pursuit for success? If you're a mobster and your only concern is to win at all costs, Machiavelli is your man. If you're anyone else on the planet, you should be with Solomon. If you are still straddling the fence, let's explore the matter further. Your "yes" or "no" answers to a few simple questions below are required. Just so you are clear on the views of our two sages, I have included quotes from each related to the question. As a rule of thumb, Machiavelli would answer "Yes" to these questions, whereas King Solomon would say "No."

1. Do you believe that a solid bottom line is justified by whatever means are used to attain it?

Machiavelli said, "[H]e will be successful who directs his actions according to the spirit of the times." And: "[I]t is necessary for a prince wishing to hold his own to know how to do wrong, and to make use of it or not according to necessity."

Solomon said, "A fortune made by a lying tongue is a fleeting vapor and a deadly snare."

If a Machiavellian endorses a policy where the ends justify the means in ruling a republic, is it impractical to believe he would not endorse the same policy in operating a business? You live by one set of values, not an assortment from which to choose in different situations. A Machiavellian believes it's okay to do wrong, whatever that might be, whenever it serves his interests: cook the books, lie on an application to secure funds, falsify a financial statement or a tax return, or deceive his shareholders. Almost anything goes if it helps to achieve the desired result.

Solomon's not having any. He wrote that it is detestable to break the law, which means he would not file a false tax return or lie on a bank statement. He believed that money gained through dishonest measures is wrong in any circumstance, so he would never have deceived his shareholders, inflated his expenses, or defrauded his company. King Solomon doesn't provide for any conditions that would justify such behavior.

2. Do you believe that situations arise in business that justify employing dishonest business tactics?

Machiavelli said, "The promise given was a necessity of the past: the word broken is a necessity of the present." And: "No enterprise is more likely to succeed than one concealed from the enemy until it is ripe for execution." And: "Men are so simple and yield so readily to the desires of the moment that he who will trick will always find another who will suffer to be tricked." And finally: "It is double pleasure to deceive the deceiver."

Solomon disagreed. "Better a poor man whose walk is blameless than a fool whose lips are perverse." And: "The LORD detests lying lips, but he delights in men who are truthful." And: "A lying tongue hates those it hurts, and a flattering mouth works ruin." And: "Truthful lips endure forever, but a lying tongue lasts only a moment." And finally: "Dishonest money dwindles away, but he who gathers money little by little makes it grow."

A Machiavellian believes the ends justify the means. Deceptive practices are okay if they help you gain an advantage over your competitor. Misleading advertisement is acceptable. Deceptive labor practices are acceptable. A strategically placed bribe or payoff is acceptable. Anything goes if you can get away with it, and it helps your business to one-up the competition. What's more, a Machiavellian believes it is okay to repay dishonesty with further dishonesty and, in taking it a step further, gets pleasure out of it. He would have no problem spreading false rumors about a competitor or a colleague who wronged him, or a supplier who overcharged him for product. He appears to have little regard for people in general and will resort to deceptive measures to return an injustice against him.

A follower of Solomon's way does not repay an injustice with a further injustice. He deals with it appropriately and wisely. He will not spread false rumors or file a fraudulent lawsuit to get even with a party that wronged him. He never resorts to conniving business practices to gain an advantage over his competitors. He will not resort to any practice in his business that allows him to obtain money dishonestly. Further, he will not let the dishonest action of another cause him to compromise the high standards under which he operates his business.

3. In dealing with your competitors, is it acceptable to do whatever is necessary to gain an advantage, even if it means driving them out of business?

Machiavelli would say yes. "[M]en ought either to be well treated or crushed, because they can avenge themselves of lighter injuries, of more serious ones they cannot, therefore the injury that is to be done to a man ought to be of such a kind that one does not stand in fear of revenge." And: "Whoever conquers a free town and does not demolish it commits a great error and may expect to be ruined himself."

But Solomon taught, "Do not gloat when your enemy falls; when he stumbles, do not let your heart rejoice, or the LORD will see and disapprove and turn his wrath away from him." And: "He who plots evil will be known as a schemer." And: "Do not exploit the poor because they are poor and do not crush the needy in court, for the LORD will take up their case and will plunder those who plunder them."

A Machiavellian will take no prisoners in his efforts to destroy competition. Being better isn't enough. He wants his competition to sleep with the fishes. He'll do whatever is necessary to become the last business left standing.

Not so with a follower of Solomon. He refuses to plot evil against the competition or engage in cruel tactics in an effort to compete with them. He competes honestly and aboveboard. He is satisfied to gain an advantage but will not resort to malicious attacks to annihilate his competitors.

4. In dealing with your employees, is it more effective to be well thought of and respected, or feared and respected?

Machiavelli wrote, "It is much safer to be feared than to be loved if of one of the two has to be lacking." And: "Men have less hesitation about offending one who makes himself loved than one who makes himself feared." And: "It is of the greatest advantage in a republic to have laws that keep her citizens poor."

Solomon wrote, "He who seeks good finds goodwill, but evil comes to him who searches for it." And: "He who is kind to the poor lends to the LORD, and he will reward him for what he has done." And: "He who oppresses the poor shows contempt for their Maker, but whoever is kind to the needy honors God."

A Machiavellian does not have the best interests of his employees at heart. It's all about security in being a feared employer or supervisor rather than one who is loved. He doesn't believe in sharing the wealth, and finds an advantage in keeping his employees needy and dependent on his business.

A follower of Solomon, on the other hand, treats his employees with dignity and respect. He does not take advantage of them. He believes God will reward him for treating his workers fairly. He would much rather be loved than feared.

5. Does integrity matter, and is it acceptable to compromise yours when doing so serves the interests of your business?

Machiavelli said, "And if, to be sure, sometimes you need to conceal a fact with words, do it in such a way that it does not become known, or, if it does become known, that you have a ready and quick defense." And: "A prince never lacks legitimate reasons to break his promise." And: "When an error is very generally adopted, I believe it to be advantageous often to refute it." And: "A man who wishes to act entirely up to his professions of virtue soon meets with what destroys him among so much that is evil." And: "A wise ruler ought never to keep faith when by doing so it would be against his interests."

Solomon said, "The man of integrity walks securely, but he who takes crooked paths will be found out." And: "The integrity of the upright guides them, but the unfaithful are destroyed by duplicity." And: "He who pursues righteousness and love finds life, prosperity and honor."

A Machiavellian is manipulative and cunning. He is concerned with integrity only to the extent that he is perceived by others to have it, when in fact he has none. That's how he operates his business.

For a follower of Solomon, his integrity is real, consistent, and paramount. You can see it in the way he lives his life and operates his business. The billionaire founder and chairman of Chick-fil-A, S. Truett Cathy, says it best: "People and principles before profit." He's been running his business that way for over half a century. Integrity matters.

You Gotta Choose

Who's it going to be? Solomon or Machiavelli? Machiavelli or Solomon? You have to choose. I realize that choosing can be hard. But you can't cheat yourself by not knowing who you're really with. And in the end, that's like siding with Machiavelli, without being brave enough to own your decision.

In 1989, Edward McDonald was the head of the Organized Crime Strike Force in the Eastern District of New York. He came to visit me while I was in prison. It had become public that I was walking away from the mob, and word was out on the street that I was marked for death by the Colombo family. Carmine Persico Jr., the family boss, was extremely upset with me for my defection, and the contract to kill me had been issued. There was even a rumor going around that my legendary father had been given the contract. The strike force chief was accompanied by two special agents of the FBI.

To them it looked like a simple deal. Since I had renounced the life, they wanted me to cooperate with the government against my former associates. I was offered protection and a chance to begin a new life under a new identity. And all I had to do was testify in a number of major mob trials—in other words, violate trust in an untold number of ways to an untold number of persons. I was reluctant. It's not what I wanted to do. I held no animosity against my former associates. I walked away from the life for different reasons. The meeting lasted for less than an hour, and the G-men knew I wasn't at all anxious to join their team.

I will never forget the words McDonald said to me as the meeting was about to end. He leaned over the table, looked me square in the eye, and said, "Michael, you have no options. As of right now, you're a dead man." The look in his eyes told me the few seconds of silence that followed were not meant simply for effect. McDonald really believed I was just that—a dead man!

I needed him to tell me that? Like I hadn't been in the life long enough to know that my former associates would be coming for me? I was in trouble, all right. Serious trouble! I knew that. But you can't let the forecast box you in. No one knows the future. I wasn't a dead man yet. I was still breathing. I still had a pulse. And contrary to what McDonald and the agents believed, I did have options. Sometimes you can't deny the diagnosis, but you can deny the outcome. I wasn't quite sure what my options were at the time, but since I never testified against any of my former mobster associates—and I am not pounding on the keys of my computer from the grave—it is quite obvious that I did have some alternatives. I am very fortunate to have chosen what I believe to be the right one.

> Carefully consider the path for your feet, and all your ways will be established.
>
> SOLOMON

Don't let the circumstances rob you of your power to choose. Are you willing to compromise to pull out that fourth quarter, bend the rules to get a contract, spin the truth to make the sale? You gotta choose. Machiavelli on one shoulder, Solomon on the other. Choose.

But think about this: You don't really know how anything's going to shake out in the long run. On the other hand, you do have to live with yourself and the consequences of your decisions every minute of the rest of your life. If that's all you know for sure, the choice is simple. That deal looks so ripe you'll do anything to land it? Don't fool yourself. It could all come undone in your face, a week, a month, a year later. You don't have a lock on the future, and the forecast is a guess. It may be a better bet than Honeydew in the fourth, but it's still a bet. Do the right thing. You don't control the future, but you can still live at peace in the present by making the right choice.

GET THE MESSAGE

1. You can't have it both ways. You're either with Machiavelli or you're with Solomon. Do you want to run your business with an "end justifies the means' approach or with integrity?

2. Don't let the circumstances rob you of your power to choose. Are you willing to compromise to pull out that fourth quarter win, bend the rules to get a contract, or spin the truth to make a sale?

CHAPTER ELEVEN

Get the Right Idea About Success

Success means different things to different people. In business, success usually comes down to the bottom line. Profits determine success, and the more profit the business generates, the greater its measure.

In La Cosa Nostra success is determined by the accumulation of wealth and the attainment of position. Its formula is simple:

$$money + position = power$$

Power in that life is viewed as the ultimate achievement of success. My dad, although spending more than thirty years in prison, will tell you he is a successful mobster. He rose in the ranks from soldier to caporegime to underboss, and he made more than a few bucks along the way. He is now considered the elder statesman of the Colombo family, time-tested and well-respected. As of this writing, he is ninety-two years old. Yes, he is still on parole, and even worse, he was charged in a new federal racketeering indictment recently returned against members of the Colombo family. It is quite possible my dad will breathe his last breath from behind bars. Is he successful? He's my dad.

I love him, but I would have preferred he had a little less "success" and a lot more freedom over the past thirty-eight years.

When I was inducted into the Colombo family, success for me was simple: pull as much money as possible. I made plenty of it, which led to my being elevated to a position of authority and procuring a considerable amount of power. As far as organized crime was concerned, I was a success. And I did it Machiavelli-style. He said that "a prince ought, above all things, always to endeavour in every action to gain for himself the reputation of being a great and remarkable man." Mob guys to a tee.

Stuffing Sausage

Success is not necessarily bound by the morality of the achiever or by the quality of his or her endeavors. It's got nothing to do with career path and profession. You can be a successful doctor, lawyer, or Indian chief. Or you can succeed in bank robbery, burglary, and murder. A dictionary definition of success says it's "the favorable or prosperous termination of attempts or endeavours." If a person accomplishes his or her goals in pursuit of his or her objectives, then that indivual is successful by definition. But dictionary definitions are like sausage casings. It all depends on what you stuff inside. If you want success that means something to you, then you'd better get your ingredients straight before you start stuffing.

Solomon's perspective was pretty balanced. He wrote, "He who pursues righteousness and love finds life, prosperity and honor." He believed success was realized in the fulfillment of leading a righteous life, reaping the rewards of prosperity, and being viewed as honorable by God and man. Nowadays that sounds right to me. As a made man, that sounded like sucker talk.

Most of the money I earned was through mob-related schemes. I made millions of dollars, but along with the bundles of cash came a barrel of troubles in the form of intense scrutiny from law enforcement, grand jury subpoenas, indictments, federal and state trials, a prison sentence, and so much more. I accumulated substantial wealth. I owned a Lear jet, a helicopter, and beautiful homes in New York, California, and Florida. I worked fifteen and eighteen hours a day in pursuit of my success and, in the process, deprived my family of precious and quality time spent with them. My success became a snowball, rolling down an endless mountainside, turning into an avalanche. Sound familiar?

Looking back, I can honestly say that despite all the money, possessions, and prestige I accumulated, I was severely lacking in the quality of my life. In that regard, I was definitely not successful. I stuffed the sausage with all the wrong ingredients. And when it aged and ripened like a nice salami, I wasn't prepared to stomach that taste.

Life is all about the ingredients.

> Don't wear yourself out to get rich; stop giving your attention to it. As soon as your eyes fly to it, it disappears, for it makes wings for itself and flies like an eagle to the sky.
>
> SOLOMON

Look where the tireless pursuit of riches got Bernie Ebbers. Look where it got our whole financial system! Riches grow wings.

Don't allow your business pursuits to infringe upon the quality of your life—yours or your family's. The continuous pursuit of wealth and prestige always adds a sour taste to life.

There almost certainly will come a time when you take your business as far as it can go in terms of earnings. When attempting to take your company beyond its capacity to earn may cost more than it will return to you in the form of profit. When the time you are investing won't pay dividends. When it robs you of your chance to enjoy life as a result of your efforts. Burnout, failure, and other things, such as divorce and bad health are the denominations in which that sort of pursuit pays its investors.

Some of you reading this book are in that situation right now. Be smart! Back up and take a hard look at the direction you are taking your business. Is it worth it? Will it pay off? Be in control of the business; don't let the business control you. Don't mistake hard work for wasted energy. Trust me: I speak from experience. I made the mistake of staying in the game too long and was no better for it. All the money in the world isn't of any benefit if you don't take time to enjoy it.

My personal road to achieving success in business is better described as a journey that led me through a maze of twists and turns, ups and downs, triumphs and defeats, with rarely, if ever, a dull moment along the way. And somehow, in some way and for some reason, I am still standing. At least I was as of this writing. Achieving success in business is rarely an easy task, and maintaining that success for a meaningful period of time can be even more challenging, despite what all the business gurus are telling you in their airport books and late-night television infomercials.

There is no secret. There are no guarantees. You know the

drill. Get an idea and work a plan around it. Get the right sort of people to help you execute your plan. Play it smart and play it ethically (no point being rich if you can't sleep at night). The rest is up to God and the market (and don't go confusing those two).

Weigh the Cost

In the years following my release from prison, I tried and failed in three different attempts to succeed in business. I couldn't shake off the rust from the inactivity of the nearly eight years I spent in prison. I still had a number of financial issues to deal with that plagued me for years as a result of my multiple racketeering indictments in the mid-1980s. There was also the matter of resolving my court-ordered fine and restitution, and the IRS was hounding me for a ton in back taxes. Add that to the grossly inflated cost of living in Southern California and providing for a family of six. I just couldn't get myself off the dime financially.

I made several bad decisions and misfires in pursuit of creating a viable business venture that would meet the financial needs of my family. I began to view myself as a one-hit wonder, having made a chart-busting rise to infamy and fortune in the mob, only to fizzle out and fail to make a decent living in the real world. There was a point in time where it was becoming increasingly difficult for me to resist the urge to resort to my old Machiavellian way of doing business, the way in which I thrived and prospered.

My vocation and business today was in no way planned. A speaker? Author? Gimme a break, right? It didn't develop overnight. It evolved over time. Gradually, my new business was beginning to enjoy an ever-increasing level of financial success, along with the realization that the people I addressed were benefiting from the information I had to share. The Machiavellian philosophy I once adhered to was about exploiting people for personal advantage, rather than sharing knowledge so that everyone, myself included, could benefit.

> The righteous man is rescued from trouble, and it comes on the wicked instead.
>
> SOLOMON

Will I ever reach the level of financial success with my current line that I did with my former? I doubt it. And I'm not concerned with that. I'm working with better ingredients these days. So what if the salami is smaller—it's more savory than anything I was making before. I am alive and free and privileged to be building a business that will hopefully provide for the quality of life I would like my family and me to enjoy, along with the added bonus of it making a difference in the lives of others. I have been blessed with that opportunity, while most all of my Machiavellian former counterparts are either dead or in jail for the remainder of their natural lives.

Take time to reevaluate your idea of success. Sweeter and richer are not always mutually inclusive. Do you have time to spend with your family? In pursuits you enjoy? With the friends you cherish? Can you give to those in need? The offer you can't refuse is your ability to refuse a raw deal. If your idea of success is cheating you out of your life, you need to make some changes.

That might not mean you're going to make the most money, but it could very well mean you're going to live without pressing financial burdens, you're going to be happier, and you're going to sleep better at night than the guy earning millions. We all know it: making the most money or operating the largest company in the world does not cut a straight line to an extraordinary quality of life. The list of wealthy entrepreneurs who died in misery and without friends or family by their sides is a lengthy one. Be sure you are not counted among them.

GET THE MESSAGE

1. Success is all about the ingredients—it all depends on what you stuff inside. If you want success that means something to you, then you'd better get your ingredients straight before you start stuffing.

2. Have you taken your business as far as it can go? Don't mistake hard work for wasted energy. Back up and take a hard look at the direction you are taking your business. Is it worth it? Will it pay off? Achieving success in your business is rarely an easy task, and maintaining that success for a meaningful period of time can be even more challenging.

3. Take time to reevaluate your idea of success. Sweeter and richer are not always mutually inclusive. If your idea of success is cheating you out of your life, you need to make some changes.

Closing Thoughts

H e will get whacked!" That's a quote from Special Agent Bernie Welsh of the FBI upon his hearing that I was quitting the mob. "I wouldn't want to be in Michael Franzese's shoes. I don't think his life expectancy is very substantial," added Ed McDonald, former strike force chief of the Eastern District of New York, who was no less confident in my ability to survive the mob's death sentence. The night I took the oath to become a made man, I was one of six recruits inducted into the family. I am the only one alive today. None of them died of natural causes. I'm not the smartest businessperson alive today. Nor am I the most successful. But you can consider me to be among those who have been the most tried and tested and quite possibly, one of the most resourceful. I have been counted out more times than a punch-drunk club fighter. I earned my master's degree in business, and in life, not from college, but from the school of hard knocks—and have managed to succeed in both, where most of my contemporaries have not. I've got "staying power."

Staying power should never be overlooked when evaluating a person's long-term success. It's a character trait that most successful businesspeople possess. Staying power is what enables you to take the inevitable falls that come with running a business and still end up landing on your feet.

With staying power comes experience, and the tips I have shared with you are a result of my many years of it. I consider myself to be extremely fortunate—blessed to be alive and free to share these tips with you. Follow them and your road to success in both business and life will be a lot less hazardous.

It should not take a horse's head to convince you that I have made you an offer you should not refuse.

The Broken Business of Government

NEW FOR THIS EDITION

A mobster defines "business" as almost any activity in which a person or a group of people engages that somehow and in some way generates money. It could be legal or illegal, for profit, nonprofit, a corporation, a cartel, a partnership, a family, or a church. Doesn't matter. As long as the entity's activities are raking in money, in the view of most mobsters that entity is a business. And as far as the mob is concerned, the government's activities are one big money-raking business.

Spend enough time in a mob social club, and you'll get an earful about the business of government and the politicians who run it.

"Fat Tony" Salerno, Carmine "the snake" Persico, Paul "Big Paul" Castellano, and even the Dapper Don himself, John Gotti, at one time or another would circle a card table, sipping black coffee with a shot of anisette, and roast our elected officials like there was no tomorrow. "Washington would be rolling over in his grave if he saw the way these bums operate today." "The thieves would all be in front of a firing squad." And—no joke, now—"They call us gangsters; they're the real gangsters."

The general consensus of these executives is that the current era of government officials are more concerned with lining their own pockets and enriching their own lives than they are in serving the public who voted them into office. Being the constant target of federal RICO indictments tends to stir up some strong emotional responses in a man. Mobsters are also quick to compare the government to their own operations, saying, "The Feds operate more like a mob bugatta than we do." I've heard it a thousand times that Uncle Sam operates like La Cosa Nostra. I'm actually going to look at that idea in a future book. Stay tuned. But what about government as a business? Before you dismiss the mobsters' view, take a closer look.

A business exists to sell a product or to provide a service. The government is mainly in the service business. It provides services to its citizens and others who reside within its borders—as is the case for some twelve million illegal aliens who have taken up residence here, but that's another issue for another time. For those services, the government collects a fee in the form of a wide assortment of taxes.

Historically, the government also offers products to consumers, but it's more of a sideline, consisting primarily of property seized by law enforcement in criminal and civil prosecutions or military surplus items. More recently, though, government has shown interest in owning and operating other businesses, banks, and automakers, for instance—but that's also another discussion for another time.

Like the complaining mobsters, we all know that government is a broken business.

Most of the tips I provide here are not employed by the politicians in charge—and it shows. Congress would be far more efficient conducting its business in a sit-down; heaven help the representative who endorsed a bill he had never read, or the one who dared to go off at his contemporary in an angry tirade. Obama should have done better in choosing his consiglieres. Appointing a tax evader to oversee the Treasury? I don't think so. You don't appoint a gambler to oversee the bookmaking operation. Come on. And does Nancy Pelosi think before she talks? Like Solomon said, even fools look smart if they keep their mouth shut. Put a lid on it already.

It's about time the shareholders of the business of government have a sit-down with the people in charge. It's time to put our public servants on the carpet—both our elected and appointed officials—and see if they're really serving us or themselves, see if they're working within the framework the founders set up to benefit all Americans or if they're just working within their own framework of ambitions for the benefit of themselves and their cronies and backers.

A Model In Need of Repair

I stated in Chapter Two that mobsters believe the money in another person's pocket really belongs to them. They also believe that the best way to fund a business is to do so by the OPM method, with *other people's money.* Sound familiar? The business of government is funded entirely with other people's money. Your money! Every program, every agency, every entitlement, and every barrel of pork, along with the salaries of those who order it up, are paid for with other people's money.

And therein lies the problem with the government business

model. Unlike the owners of a private business, CEOs in the business of government don't take a financial loss when the business does. They don't have to answer to a board of directors or some angry shareholders for their bad decisions. They don't have to face a relative or friend whose hard-earned money they squandered by making a bad investment or mismanaging the business. Heck, they don't even get a cut in pay.

When was the last time members of congress took a pay cut? Forget about that—when was the first time? Government-run programs have lost more taxpayer money than an army of Bernie Madoffs, yet in almost every instance those in charge are not required to answer for it, not really. Because the politicians are spending our money, not their own, voters have to elect responsible and moral people to manage our affairs, who will treat your money like it is their own. In my view, in financially challenging times such as these, we need people who have some experience with running a business. If you've struggled to meet a payroll and have had to be prudent with expenses, then you know what I'm getting at. So many of the people now running the nation's business don't know jack about that. And it shows like a black eye.

The business of the United States is in debt to the tune of almost fifteen trillion dollars, and that debt is growing daily. The vig paid on that debt was over four hundred billion dollars in fiscal year 2010 alone. Basically, the business of our nation is broke.

And how do our national CEOs, CFOs, and COOs handle this avalanche of debt? They just borrow more money and shift the burden to those paying their salaries today and in the future. Rather than placing a limit on their spending, the guys in charge continue to raise the statutory limit under which the business of government can borrow. What did Solomon say about this kind of behavior? "Do not be a man who strikes hands in a pledge or puts up security for debts; if you lack the means to pay your very bed will be snatched from under you." At the rate our government is borrowing money and accumulating debt, we all better get accustomed to sleeping on a couch made in China.

This isn't rocket science. A couple of meatheads standing on the corner know this much. A business cannot borrow itself out of debt unless the money it borrows is used to turn a profit that will allow it to pay down its debt. The smart mobsters don't borrow shylock money to pay off a debt and then get saddled with five-point weekly vig, unless they're going to use the money to make a score. Mobsters don't borrow from Peter to pay Paul. They borrow from Carmine "the snake" or Harry "the hat." And those guys know how to collect their money. Growing debt to pay down debt is a sure path to destruction, unless you cut spending and increase cash flow. The politicians aren't doing either. And if they are, it's not nearly enough.

And don't fall for the tax trap. Tax collections are at an all time low because people are out of work. Raising taxes is not going to cut it this time around. How much higher can we raise them, anyway? The United States already has the highest corporate tax rate in the world. If our nation's business is once again going to become profitable (have a surplus, not a deficit), then our leaders must begin to act responsibly and treat the business of government as if it were funded by their own money and not yours. It's not brain surgery. They need to do four things:

1. *Cut spending.* Difficult, but absolutely necessary. Our leaders need to stop talking about it and actually do it. And they

need to be honest about it. They need to stop proposing spending cuts in one area while secretly pushing through expensive pork projects and new programs in another. Shell game finances need to stop.

They need to drastically reduce or eliminate entitlement programs that are crippling us with debt. I would love to see every citizen of our country have affordable health care, myself included. But right now, we can't afford it. We're broke. The issue is not how good or bad the bill is; that's another discussion. The issue is how costly it is. We can talk all day long about how effective, necessary, and helpful the program is, but the simple fact is we don't have enough lettuce for the salad. The healthcare bill needs to be repealed and the issue revisited when we can actually pay for it. It was totally irresponsible and downright dishonest for our leaders to vote a costly healthcare bill into law at a time when there is no conceivable way to pay for it. You don't expand the business if the business isn't pulling its weight. The same is true of all our entitlement programs. If we cannot afford to pay for it, the benefits are irrelevant.

What they need to do is trim it all back, decrease the size of government. The bigger the government, the more it costs *you*. By expanding government all we do is increase the nation's overhead without really increasing the cash flow. In most cases, a government-run program is significantly inferior to a similar program run by the private sector. I was amazed to learn that the Russian mob alone is responsible for defrauding Medicare out of over sixty billion dollars a year. The same Russian mob partnered with me many years ago to defraud the government out of billions in taxes in the gasoline industry—right under the eyes of those government workers running the program. Can any business survive such a massive amount of fraud? How long before the program collapses under the weight of its own inefficiency? We all know that Social Security is in dire straits. How many more government-run programs are on life support? My guess—most all of them.

Don't get me started on unionized government workers. I know a thing about unions. Every additional benefit won by a union for a government worker comes out of your pocket, and it isn't doing the country any good. All they do is jack up the price of business.

Congress can create a law eliminating government unions and create a pay scale for its workers in line with the jobs they perform and the skill level they have achieved. As it stands now, federal government workers earn higher wages than workers in the private sector performing the same type of work. They enjoy more pay increases then union workers in the private sector. And most often receive better benefits. The unions are hurting the private sector on the one hand (look at GM) and hurting taxpayers on the other. We need to eliminate the unions for government workers. Period.

Those in charge of running the business of government need to follow my advice: Do what government does best and eliminate the rest. Protect our borders. Operate the schools. Enforce the laws that are necessary to maintain order on the streets. Help fund research projects that will improve the lives of all Americans. These are necessary and meaningful functions of the business of our nation. Stop wasting money on the rest.

2. Increase cash flow. Not by raising taxes on the wealthy or on corporate America. We need to get people back to work so everyone can pay their fair share of taxes, not just the top one percent of those who live here. Raising taxes on the wealthy encourages them to seek safe havens for their money elsewhere rather than to stimulate our economy by spending it within our nation's borders. And raising taxes on corporate America causes those companies to reduce costs by expanding their operations overseas rather than within our borders.

3. Eliminate borrowing. This should be a no-brainer. No further explanation is necessary. Those in charge of our nation's business need to realize that they can't keep raising the debt ceiling and counterfeiting money. The borrowing must stop. Before long, the wolf is going to be at the door, and by all accounts he will be dressed in a silk robe.

4. Enforce the laws against illegal aliens. So maybe it's not another issue for another time. I know that this issue has been beaten to death and politicized even further. But there is no viable reason for our government to fail to enforce the federal laws that already exist against those aliens who enter and reside in our country illegally. Illegal aliens are a tremendous drain on an already broken economy. We all know the reasons why: criminal activity perpetrated by some; the drain on an already over burdened health-care system; the cost to educate their children in our public schools. The list goes on. And yet law enforcement agents who attempt to enforce the laws against illegal aliens are demonized, accused of being racist and of engaging in racial profiling. This needs to stop. Enforcing the laws against illegal immigrants is a vital step to getting the business of our nation back in order.

Cut to the Chase

In the business of government, as in the private sector, there is no quick fix or secret formula to achieve success. And granted, the business of government is a complicated one. But someone has to do it, and the American people have to act wisely and responsibly when choosing a candidate for office that will be entrusted with doing his or her part in managing the business of our nation. We will never get it right until we get the right people managing the store. Those people, the Solomons, are out there, and we'd better pray that they emerge ready to conduct the hard business of the people. Right now, we're mostly led by Machiavellians. And we cannot long endure that.

Acknowledgments

To my agent, friend, and "consigliere," Esther, for all of her efforts and advice. Without her, this book would not have been possible.

To Joel Miller, my "Underboss," for allowing the book to go the distance, and for his valuable guidance throughout the process.

To my daughter, Julia, who volunteered the use of her laptop when mine went to sleep with the fishes.

To my beautiful wife and partner for life, Camille, who keeps me grounded in the reality that I am far more blessed than good. She is my rock!

To God who has so mercifully blessed me with a second opportunity to succeed in this life. Without Him, I would have been neither alive nor free to complete this project or any other. To Him goes all the glory!

About the Author

Michael Franzese, until just a few years ago, was one of the biggest money earners the mob had seen since Al Capone, and the youngest individual on *Fortune* magazine's survey of "The Fifty Biggest Mafia Bosses." At one point he was earning millions every week. After the last in a series of racketeering indictments, however, Michael decided to plead guilty, accept a 10-year prison sentence, and quit the mob.

Franzese is now a man on a mission. Determined to use the compelling experiences of his former life for the benefit of at-risk youth, professional and student athletes, corporate executives, and for anyone seeking the inspiration to beat the odds and make positive changes in their lives, he has become a highly regarded motivational speaker and a source of invaluable information.

For more information and to stay in touch with Michael, you can connect with him here:

www.MichaelFranzese.com

 @MichaelFranzese

 Michael Franzese Ministries